Praise for Arise My Soul

Gary Holloway has captured the hymns of Charles Wesley in a very creative way. This devotional collection of Wesley's not only strikes a chord of sweet memories, but it also brings them forward and expands on their spiritual significance for our life today.
—**Jackie Patillo**, President of the *Gospel Music Association*

***

Charles Wesley's hymnic corpus is a gift that keeps giving. After nearly 300 years in circulation, his hymns continue to be a wellspring of spiritual nourishment. This book unpacks the message of his hymns in an approachable and pastoral manner, a resource worth keeping on any hymn lover's bookshelf.
—**Chris Fenner**, Editor, *Hymnology Archive*

***

For almost 250 years, the hymns of Charles Wesley have continued to shape and form people increasingly into the image of Christ. This wonderful volume from Gary Holloway takes us deeper into this rich treasure trove of hymns that are worthy of passing on to the next generation. May it help us follow Wesley's call to "keep an eye toward God as we sing…heartily and with good courage!"
—**Dr. D.J. Bulls**, Hymnologist & Worship Leader, *Tyler, TX*

***

Arise My Soul is a compelling mixture of beautiful hymns from Charles Wesley with reflections on God's Word, blended with rich theology. In these daily meditations the heart is lifted before our Creator as He continues to write the song of our Lord Jesus within us, to sing for the world around us. What a wonderful treasure from Dr. Gary Holloway.
—**Danny Gregg**, Worship Minister, *Donelson Church of Christ, Nashville, Tennessee*

Arise My Soul

Forty Days with Charles Wesley

BY
Gary Holloway

Published by KHARIS PUBLISHING, an imprint of KHARIS MEDIA LLC.
Copyright © 2025 Gary Holloway
ISBN-13: 978-1-63746-364-2
ISBN-10: 1-63746-364-2
Library of Congress Control Number: 2025945732

All rights reserved. This book or parts thereof may not be reproduced in any form, stored in a retrieval system, or transmitted in any form by any means - electronic, mechanical, photocopy, recording, or otherwise - without prior written permission of the publisher, except as provided by United States of America copyright law.

Unless otherwise noted, all Scripture references are from the Holy Bible, New Living Translation, copyright ©1996, 2004, 2015 by Tyndale House Foundation. Used by permission of Tyndale House Publishers, Carol Stream, Illinois 60188. All rights reserved.

Scripture quotations marked ESV are from the ESV® Bible (The Holy Bible, English Standard Version®), copyright © 2001 by Crossway Bibles, a publishing ministry of Good News Publishers. Used by permission. All rights reserved.

Scripture quotation marked NIV is taken from the Holy Bible, New International Version®, NIV® Copyright © 1973, 1978, 1984, 2011 by Biblica, Inc. Used with permission. All rights reserved worldwide.

All KHARIS PUBLISHING products are available at special quantity discounts for bulk purchases for sales promotions, premiums, fund-raising, and educational needs. For details, contact:

Kharis Media LLC
Tel: 1-630-909-3405
support@kharispublishing.com
www.kharispublishing.com

CONTENTS

Introduction 7

Day One: *Come, Let us Anew* 9

Day Two: *Come, Thou Long Expected Jesus* 13

Day Three: *Hark! The Herald Angels Sing* 17

Day Four: *Jesus, Lord, We Look to Thee* 21

Day Five: *Come, Let us Use the Grace Divine (I)* 25

Day Six: *Come, Let us Use the Grace Divine (II)* 28

Day Seven: *Jesus, Lover of my Soul* 31

Day Eight: *Come, Holy Spirit, From on High (I)* 36

Day Nine: *Come, Holy Spirit, From on High (II)*. 39

Day Ten: *Forth in Your Name* 42

Day Eleven: *Christ, Whose Glory Fills the Skies* 47

Day Twelve: *O For a Heart to Praise my God* 50

Day Thirteen: *Jesus, Thine All-Victorious Love* 55

Day Fourteen: *Soldiers of Christ, Arise (I)* 59

Day Fifteen: *Soldiers of Christ, Arise (II)* 62

Day Sixteen: *Let Earth and Heaven Agree* 66

Day Seventeen: *Weary of Wandering From my God* 71

Day Eighteen: *Jesus, My Truth, My Way* 75

Day Nineteen: *All Praise to our Redeeming Lord (I)* 79

Day Twenty: *All Praise to our Redeeming Lord (II)* 82

Day Twenty-One: *Blow ye the Trumpet, Blow (I)* 85

Day Twenty-Two: *Blow ye the Trumpet, Blow* (II)..............89

Day Twenty-Three: *You Servants of God* 93

Day Twenty-Four: *And Can it Be* 97

Day Twenty-Five: *O Love Divine, What Hast Thou Done?*102

Day Twenty-Six: *'Tis Finished!*..105

Day Twenty-Seven: *Arise my Soul, Arise (I)* 109

Day Twenty-Eight: *Arise My Soul, Arise (II)*....................112

Day Twenty-Nine: *Forever Here My Rest Shall Be* 115

Day Thirty: *Christ the Lord is Risen Today (I)* 119

Day Thirty-One: *Christ the Lord is Risen Today (II)*.........122

Day Thirty-Two: *Jesus Christ is Risen* 125

Day Thirty-Three: *Come, Let us Join With One Accord*....128

Day Thirty-Four: *I Know That my Redeemer Lives (I)* 133

Day Thirty-Five: *I Know That my Redeemer Lives (II)*......136

Day Thirty-Six: *Love Divine (I)*..139

Day Thirty-Seven: *Love Divine (II)* 142

Day Thirty-Eight: *O For a Thousand Tongues to Sing (I)*.145

Day Thirty-Nine: *O For a Thousand Tongues to Sing (II)* 148

Day Forty: *A Charge to Keep* 152

Introduction

Charles Wesley (1707-1788) is perhaps the most famous English language hymn writer of all time. At any moment in any country of the world, Christians are singing one of the over 6500 hymns he wrote. Along with his older brother, John Wesley (1703-1791), Charles was a founder of the Methodist movement in the Church of England. While John had worldwide influence as a preacher and theologian, Charles moved the hearts of millions through his spiritual poems put to music.

This book gives you a way to experience daily these powerful lyrics, some familiar and some you may not have known. Each day begins with a stanza from a hymn, followed by a passage from the Bible that reflects the hymn. A brief meditation on the words of the hymn and the scripture follows to lead you deeper into communion with God. After contemplation of all the stanzas for that day, questions follow to prompt thought and discussion. Then there are suggestions on how to let the power of the hymn shape your life today. A brief prayer follows.

Wesley's hymns predominantly centered on the life, death, resurrection, and glorification of Jesus as the Messiah. The sequence of hymns in this book generally follows the same direction, focusing on what God the Father is doing for His people through Jesus the Son and the Holy Spirit. Even if you have sung the words of Charles Wesley for years, you may find stanzas and hymns that are new to you. You might even find deeper meaning in familiar hymns.

God wants to be near us. Father, Son, and Spirit promise us their presence if we take the time each day to be alone with them. These daily reflections can also serve as a basis for group study. And even if you encounter God in private meditation, you join with those throughout the world and throughout almost three centuries who have experienced the love of Christ through the words of Charles Wesley.

Day One:
Come, Let us Anew

STANZA ONE

Come, let us anew our journey pursue,
Roll round with the year,
And never stand still till the Master appear.
His adorable will let us gladly fulfill,
And our talents improve
By the patience of hope and the labor of love.

SCRIPTURE

As we pray to our God and Father about you, we think of your faithful work, your loving deeds, and the enduring hope you have because of our Lord Jesus Christ (1 Thessalonians 1:3).

MEDITATION

In this hymn for the New Year, Charles Wesley echoes the biblical call to love God and our neighbor. Such love requires renewed commitment every new day and every new year. Our relationship with God and others is a long journey of service and obedience.

Even if you are not reading this at the beginning of the calendar year or the Christian year, the hymn is appropriate because we can begin the journey with Jesus anew each day.

That journey calls for more than a temporary resolution for the new year. Beyond "New Year, new me," we commit ourselves again to the work of God within us and among us. We live this year in trust that the Holy Spirit produces His fruit in us. We live this year in certain hope of the resurrection. We live this year in the enduring hope that Jesus will return and we will continue our journey with Him forever.

Stanza Two

**Our life as a dream, our time as a stream
Glide swiftly away,
And the fugitive moment refuses to stay;
For the arrow is flown and the moments are gone.
The millennial year
Presses on to our view, and eternity's here.**

Scripture

How do you know what your life will be like tomorrow? Your life is like the morning fog—it's here a little while, then it's gone (James 4:14).

Meditation

"Life is short and then you die."

I think I first read that on a bumper sticker. My reaction was, "What a cynical view of life!" But the Bible often reminds us that life is short and that death is coming. This is good news because it is not the whole story. Through the cross, Jesus defeated death. Resurrection is coming! The time when everyone recognizes the reign of Jesus—the millennium of peace and the eternity of love—is coming closer.

We do not mourn the passing of the years but rejoice in the nearness of the new heaven and earth.

STANZA THREE

**Oh, that each in the day of His coming may say,
"I have fought my way thru;
I have finished the work thou didst give me to do."
Oh, that each from his Lord may receive the glad word:
"Well and faithfully done;
Enter into my joy and sit down on my throne."**

SCRIPTURE

And now the prize awaits me—the crown of righteousness, which the Lord, the righteous Judge, will give me on the day of His return. And the prize is not just for me but for all who eagerly look forward to His appearing (2 Timothy 4:8).

MEDITATION

The new year awaits us with exciting possibilities. We also do not know what challenges and sorrows that year may bring. The clear call from Jesus is to trust Him in all circumstances, whether good or bad. At times we have to fight our way through, struggling against our pain and our doubt. As we know though, the promise of Jesus in every day of every year is that the prize of a joyful future awaits us, both now and in the life to come.

FOR REFLECTION

1. What are some ways you can live in hope for this new year?
2. How is it helpful to remember that years go quickly and life is short?
3. Why is a new year a good occasion to think about the Second Coming of Jesus?

LIVE THE HYMN

1. Make a list of all the things you hope for in the new year, then test those desires in prayer to God.

2. Commit to some daily practice that can bring you closer to God this year.

PRAYER

Jesus, you know the struggle of being human. Help us in our battles this year.

Day Two:

Come, Thou Long Expected Jesus

STANZA ONE

**Come, thou long expected Jesus,
born to set thy people free;
from our fears and sins release us,
let us find our rest in thee.**

SCRIPTURE

At that time there was a man in Jerusalem named Simeon. He was righteous and devout and was eagerly waiting for the Messiah to come and rescue Israel. The Holy Spirit was upon him and had revealed to him that he would not die until he had seen the Lord's Messiah (Luke 2:25-26).

MEDITATION

Most of us know what it is like to expect a child. The mother-to-be, her husband, family, and friends all wait with great anticipation during the nine months the mother carries the child. At times, it seems the child will never arrive.

Now imagine waiting your whole life to see a newborn. That's what Simeon did. And when that child, Jesus the Messiah, arrives, and His parents present Him at the Temple, Simeon holds Him in his arms and praises the Lord. Simeon says he can die in peace.

Now try to imagine waiting centuries for a child. That's what God's people, Israel, and all the people of the earth had done. He was certainly the long-expected Jesus!

Stanza Two

**Israel's strength and consolation,
hope of all the earth thou art;
dear desire of every nation,
joy of every longing heart.**

Scripture

You faithfully answer our prayers with awesome deeds, O God our savior. You are the hope of everyone on earth, even those who sail on distant seas (Psalm 65:5).

Meditation

Israel expected a king who would sit on the throne of David, restore the nation, and bring justice and peace. For some in Israel, it was a narrow expectation that excluded other nations.

But the Lord has always been the King of all nations. Israel was to be a light to those nations, showing the path to God. The anticipated Messiah was to reign over all the earth.

So today, even in nations where few know the Lord God, there are countless hearts that long for the peace and justice this child brings.

Stanza Three

**Born thy people to deliver,
born a child and yet a King,
born to reign in us forever,
now thy gracious kingdom bring.**

Scripture

"The Lord is my rock and my fortress and my deliverer, my God, my rock, in whom I take refuge" (2 Samuel 22:3 ESV).

Meditation

We speak of someone delivering a baby, but here that baby is born to deliver us.

He delivers us from slavery to sin. He delivers us from the oppression of unjust rulers. He delivers us from our bondage to our own wants and wishes.

And He delivers us into His kingdom. This child is the King who rules each of us and also reigns over all the rulers of the world. He brings us out of the kingdoms of tyranny and repression into His kingdom of grace.

No wonder many bowed at the feet of this long-expected King!

Stanza Four

By thine own eternal spirit
rule in all our hearts alone;
by thine all sufficient merit,
raise us to thy glorious throne.

Scripture

For he raised us from the dead along with Christ and seated us with him in the heavenly realms because we are united with Christ Jesus (Ephesians 2:6).

Meditation

The Almighty God came down from heaven to save us. "So the Word became human and made his home among us" (John 1:14). We cannot imagine the distance between that heavenly life of the Word of God and being born in a stable and laid in a manger.

Jesus came all that way down in order to lift us all the way up. By His life, death, and resurrection, He gives us His merit that is sufficient to bring us into the very throne-room of God. All He asks is that we open our hearts to His Spirit and make Him our only King. We still ask Jesus to come into our hearts.

For Reflection

1. Does the thought of the birth of Jesus thrill you as much as it must have thrilled those who first saw this baby? Why or why not?
2. How does the Holy Spirit allow Jesus to rule in our hearts?
3. What does it mean to receive the merit of Jesus?

Live the Hymn

1. Relive your own anticipation for a child to be born. Now take a few minutes to imagine the centuries of expectation that God's people had for the birth of Jesus, the Messiah.
2. Take all the oppressive thoughts, habits, and sins you have and give them to Jesus, the one who was born to deliver.

Prayer

Jesus who was expected and born long ago, come into our hearts today.

Day Three:
Hark! The Herald Angels Sing

STANZA ONE

**Hark! the herald angels sing,
"Glory to the newborn King:
peace on earth, and mercy mild,
God and sinners reconciled!"
Joyful, all ye nations, rise,
join the triumph of the skies;
with th'angelic hosts proclaim,
"Christ is born in Bethlehem!"**

SCRIPTURE

Suddenly, an angel of the Lord appeared among them, and the radiance of the Lord's glory surrounded them. They were terrified, but the angel reassured them. "Don't be afraid!" he said. "I bring you good news that will bring great joy to all people. The Savior—yes, the Messiah, the Lord—has been born today in Bethlehem, the city of David!" (Luke 2:9-11).

MEDITATION

Many significant events happened in Bethlehem. That's where Jacob buried his wife, Rachel (Genesis 35:19-20). One of the judges, Ibzan, was from Bethlehem (Judges 12:8). Naomi and Ruth, her Moabite daughter-in-law, return to Bethlehem and are helped by Boaz. Samuel goes to Bethlehem to anoint David to be king (1 Samuel 16:1-14). From that day forward, God's people called Bethlehem "the City of David."

Many years after David, the Prophet Micah says a great king will someday come from Bethlehem (Micah 5:2).

Now that day has come! That King, the long-awaited Messiah, has been born in Bethlehem. We join with angels and shepherds and all nations to herald His birth.

Stanza Two

**Christ, by highest heaven adored,
Christ, the everlasting Lord,
late in time behold him come,
offspring of the Virgin's womb:
veiled in flesh the Godhead see;
hail th'incarnate Deity,
pleased with us in flesh to dwell,
Jesus, our Immanuel.**

Scripture

So all of us who have had that veil removed can see and reflect the glory of the Lord. And the Lord—who is the Spirit—makes us more and more like Him as we are changed into His glorious image (2 Corinthians 3:18).

Meditation

The shepherds and others saw the Godhead veiled in flesh when they looked at the baby in the manger. Paul speaks of the veil that covered the face of Moses when he came down from Mount Sinai, shining with the glory of God. God is so far beyond humanity, so stunning in his glory, that humans cannot see Him and live. Yet just a glimpse of God forces Moses to veil his own face so he will not blind the Israelites.

Now God has removed the veil. We see the fullness of the Deity in the flesh. And since we are in Jesus and He in us, we reflect the glory of God. Jesus is God with us.

STANZA THREE

Hail the heaven-born Prince of Peace!
Hail the Sun of Righteousness!
Light and life to all he brings,
risen with healing in his wings.
Mild he lays his glory by,
born that we no more may die,
born to raise us from the earth,
born to give us second birth.

SCRIPTURE

Though he was God, he did not think of equality with God as something to cling to. Instead, he gave up his divine privileges; he took the humble position of a slave and was born as a human being (Philippians 2:6-7).

MEDITATION

I don't think of Jesus as mild; He seems more bold and forceful to me. The word "mild" is not found anywhere in most English translations of the Bible. Yet twice in this hymn, Wesley uses the word "mild" to describe the incarnation. The angels proclaim "mercy mild." The Prince of Peace is mild when He lays aside His glory.

Wesley uses this word to capture the amazing depth of God's love in becoming flesh. Imagine the distance between the eternal glory of God and being a helpless baby in a manger. Yet Jesus went even lower for our sakes, becoming like a condemned criminal put to death on the cross.

The mild love of God in Christ overwhelms us with its power.

For Reflection

1. Why is it significant that Jesus is born in the City of David?
2. Why would God veil or hide Himself from His people?
3. Is "mild" a good word to describe Jesus? Why or why not?

Live the Hymn

1. Imagine seeing baby Jesus in the manger.
2. Reflect the glory of the Godhead revealed in Jesus as you interact with others.

Prayer

With the angels we pray and sing, "Glory to the newborn King."

Day Four:
Jesus, Lord, We Look to Thee

Stanza One

**Jesus, Lord, we look to thee,
let us in thy name agree:
show thyself the Prince of peace;
bid all strife forever cease.**

Scripture

For a child is born to us, a son is given to us. The government will rest on his shoulders. And he will be called: Wonderful Counselor, Mighty God, Everlasting Father, Prince of Peace (Isaiah 9:6).

Meditation

There are many war movies but few peace films. You can purchase countless games of battle and war, but no peace games. War means stories of courage and exhilaration. By contrast, peace sounds boring and dull, but the whole point of war is to ensure the peace. In the days of Jesus, the mighty armies of Rome enforced the Pax Romana. The emperor imposed peace through violence.

Jesus is the Prince of Peace. He also compels peace, not through war and violence, but through the overwhelming power of the sacrificial love He displayed on the cross. By that love He conquers all the powers of hatred and war, bidding strife to forever cease.

Stanza Two

**Make us of one heart and mind,
courteous, pitiful, and kind,
lowly, meek in thought and word,
altogether like our Lord.**

Scripture

Then make me truly happy by agreeing wholeheartedly with each other, loving one another, and working together with one mind and purpose (Philippians 2:2).

Meditation

It's hard to work with people who disagree with you. After all, you are right and they are wrong! It is particularly hard in church where many believe one must be "right" on certain subjects to be right with God.

We should agree wholeheartedly with our brothers and sisters in Christ. But what if we don't? The agreement Paul recommends in this verse is celebrated in the hymn. It is not an agreement on issues or policies or biblical interpretation. It is an agreement to be like Jesus—courteous, kind, lowly, and meek. Such accord comes not through thinking alike on everything, but in showing love to all our fellow believers, even those who are "wrong."

After all, Jesus loves us even when we are wrong.

Stanza Three

**Let us for each other care,
each the other's burden bear;
to thy church the pattern give,
show how true believers live.**

Scripture

Bear one another's burdens, and so fulfill the law of Christ (Galatians 6:2).

Meditation

I grew up in a church that looked for patterns in the Bible—models for worship and doctrine. We looked for the law of Christ.

This hymn speaks of the life of Jesus as a pattern. He gave himself for others. He came to serve rather than to be served. He carried our burdens of sin, sickness, and grief. This is the law or pattern of life He shows us.

If we follow the pattern of Jesus, then we look for people we can serve this day. We take the focus off our own cares and seek to carry the heavy loads of others. Such a task seems too hard for us. And it is! But Jesus shares the burden of others with us. When we do not know how to help, when we do not feel like helping, and even when we don't think they deserve our help,

Jesus shoulders the load with us through work and prayer.

Stanza Four

Free from anger and from pride,
let us thus in God abide;
all the depths of love express,
all the heights of holiness.

Scripture

Work at living in peace with everyone, and work at living a holy life, for those who are not holy will not see the Lord (Hebrews 12:14).

Meditation

"Holy" is an all-important Bible word that our age has lost. For most people, "holy" is a bad word. I read a novel recently in which those in a small town called a man "Holy Bob" because he went to church most weeks. To them, holy meant that Bob looked down on the rest of them.

The Bible uses holiness to describe the character of God that we see in Jesus. It is the direct opposite of pride. Holiness does not make us look down on others and condemn them. Holiness shows itself in acts of love. We go out of our way to help others because we are holy. We lend them a helping hand in secret, not wanting to be seen as "holy." When we witness their self-destructive acts, we react not with anger, but with compassion, as Jesus responded to those around him.

The Holy Spirit is a Spirit of concerned action.

For Reflection
1. How does Jesus fight evil in order to bring peace?
2. What should Christians agree on?
3. What comes to mind when you think of the word "holy"?

Live the Hymn
1. Find a way to make peace between others today.
2. Show patience to your fellow Christians who are wrong on certain ideas.

Prayer
Peace-making Jesus, give us one heart in working together for you.

Day Five:
Come, Let us Use the Grace Divine (I)

Stanza One

**Come, let us use the grace divine,
and all with one accord,
in a perpetual covenant
join ourselves to Christ the Lord;**

Scripture

But now Jesus, our High Priest, has been given a ministry that is far superior to the old priesthood, for He is the one who mediates for us a far better covenant with God, based on better promises (Hebrews 8:6).

Meditation

Our world celebrates the dealmakers who can negotiate a favorable contract. Even when they break the contract and suffer no ill consequences, some praise them as shrewd.

God has made a covenant with his people through Jesus. We did not have to negotiate with the Lord. He gives us a deal that is so good we cannot believe it. It is a covenant of grace where God does all the giving.

But we must receive. When we accept His covenant through Jesus, we agree to make Him the sole ruler of our lives, our absolute Dictator and King. Even that acceptance is by grace, joining us to fellow believers and to our Lord.

Stanza Two

Give up ourselves, thru Jesus' power,
his name to glorify;
and promise, in this sacred hour,
for God to live and die.

Scripture

My old self has been crucified with Christ. It is no longer I who live, but Christ lives in me. So I live in this earthly body by trusting in the Son of God, who loved me and gave himself for me (Galatians 2:20).

Meditation

We tend to divide our lives into segments. We have our work life, our family life, and our leisure time. We also have our religious or spiritual life. That's when we attend church or read a book like this or pray.

Jesus is not satisfied with just our "spiritual" life. He will not accept part-time followers. He wants every bit of our lives—work, family, and even the "me time." Or to put it better, every minute of our lives is spiritual because we have given our all to Jesus. We have made a sacred promise, a vow, to keep covenant with Him.

Our old work, family, and play distinctions ended when we died with Him in baptism and began a new life.

Stanza Three

The covenant we this moment make
be ever kept in mind;
we will no more our God forsake,
or cast these words behind.

SCRIPTURE

The Lord leads with unfailing love and faithfulness all who keep his covenant and obey his demands (Psalm 25:10).

MEDITATION

It seems that in our present time, loyalty has no value. You can't keep up with what players are on your favorite sports team since they change teams so often. You may work for a company for over twenty years, only to be let go so that company saves money. Trouble in your marriage? Just look for a better partner.

The Lord treasures loyalty. He will keep His covenant with us no matter what. In turn, He demands that we serve Him alone. The test of that covenant loyalty is obedience to His word. This obedience is not salvation by works, but an act of gratitude for His unfailing love. God does not demand perfection from us, but He does expect our full allegiance.

The Lord calls us to be loyal to Him as He is to us.

FOR REFLECTION

1. What is a covenant?
2. What must we do to keep our covenant with the Lord?
3. Do we have a life that is separate from our spiritual life?

LIVE THE HYMN

1. At the beginning of each hour today, pray that you will dedicate yourself to God.
2. Think of ways you can show loyalty to the Lord today.

PRAYER

King Jesus, give us the power to live every moment for you.

Day Six:
Come, Let us Use the Grace Divine (II)

STANZA FOUR

**We never will throw off the fear
of God who hears our vow;
and if thou art well pleased to hear,
come down and meet us now.**

SCRIPTURE

A man who makes a vow to the Lord or makes a pledge under oath must never break it. He must do exactly what he said he would do (Numbers 30:2).

MEDITATION

Sometimes in the Bible, making a vow sounds like bargaining with God. "I will do this, Lord, if you will only do what I ask." Perhaps you have made vows like this.

Vows are solemn promises we make to the Lord. We may think we have never made such vows, but all Christians do. Baptism is a vow to keep covenant with God. When we worship, we often make vows in our songs. In a sense, our entire lives are a vow, a promise to be faithful to God.

And God hears our vows! He takes our words seriously. He listens and agrees to bless us. He also makes promises to us. His greatest vow is that He will be our God and we will be His people.

Stanza Five

**Thee, Father, Son, and Holy Ghost,
let all our hearts receive,
present with thy celestial host
the peaceful answer give;**

Scripture

I will give them hearts that recognize me as the Lord. They will be my people, and I will be their God, for they will return to me wholeheartedly (Jeremiah 24:7).

Meditation

Where is God?

It could be a childish question but it's an important one. There are several correct answers. God is in heaven. God is everywhere. God is in our hearts.

When is God near us?

All the time, except we get distracted, sometimes by temptations, but often by good activities. What we need are reminders of God. Prayer, Bible study, and reflection on our day brings to our hearts the reality of the Lord's presence. Aware that God is at work in us, we live peaceably with everyone. Like the angels at the birth of Jesus, we proclaim, "peace on earth to those with whom God is pleased" (Luke 2:14).

Stanza Six

**to each covenant the blood apply
which takes our sins away,
and register our names on high
and keep us to that day!**

Scripture

Now may the God of peace—who brought up from the dead our Lord Jesus, the great Shepherd of the sheep, and ratified an eternal covenant with his blood— may he equip you with all you need for doing his will. May he produce in you, through the power of Jesus Christ, every good thing that is pleasing to him. All glory to him forever and ever! Amen (Hebrews 13:20-21).

Meditation

God has given us an eternal covenant through the blood of Jesus. It is eternal because that covenant forgives our sins once and for all. It is eternal because the Presence of God through Christ and the Holy Spirit is with us always. It is eternal because we will one day see God face to face and be with Him forever.

In a world that is constantly changing, where nothing seems permanent, and there is little to rely on, the Lord gives us His sure and certain covenant. We know He will equip us with all we need this day and keep us until the eternal day.

For Reflection

1. What are some vows you have made to God?
2. How does awareness of God lead to being at peace with others?
3. How is the peace God gives us an eternal peace?

Live the Hymn

1. Find ways to show God's peace to others in your work this day.
2. Ask the Lord for the strength to keep the vows you have made to Him.

Prayer

Holy Trinity, fill our hearts with your peaceful Presence.

Day Seven:
Jesus, Lover of my Soul

STANZA ONE

**Jesus, lover of my soul,
let me to thy bosom fly,
while the nearer waters roll,
while the tempest still is high:
hide me, O my Saviour, hide,
till the storm of life is past;
safe into the haven guide,
O receive my soul at last.**

SCRIPTURE

Jesus responded, "Why are you afraid? You have so little faith!" Then he got up and rebuked the wind and waves, and suddenly there was a great calm (Matthew 8:26).

MEDITATION

Like you, I have been through many "tempests"—tornados, hurricanes, and floods. When the rain comes down hard and the wind blows, I'm still afraid.

"Let me to thy bosom fly" does not communicate well to us today. But if you can remember the panic you felt when you first experienced a storm as a child, then you can understand the sentiment. When the storm came we ran to the safety of our mother's embrace. We flew to her bosom.

In the same way, we run to Jesus, the one who loves in all the storms of our life.

Stanza Two

**Other refuge have I none,
hangs my helpless soul on thee;
leave, ah, leave me not alone,
still support and comfort me.
All my trust on thee is stayed,
all my help from thee I bring;
cover my defenceless head
with the shadow of thy wing.**

Scripture

He will cover you with his feathers. He will shelter you with his wings. His faithful promises are your armor and protection (Psalm 91:4).

Meditation

Vulnerable. Helpless. Desperate. Defenseless.

We don't like to feel any of those ways. We like to think we are in charge and have it all together.

But we must admit there are times when we feel like frail baby birds looking for protection under the wings of our mother.

When helpless, the promises of God through Christ armor us against anything that life may throw against us. All the loving Jesus asks of us is that we trust in those promises and let Him throw His protective wing over us.

Stanza Three

**Thou, O Christ, art all I want;
more than all in thee I find;
raise the fallen, cheer the faint,
heal the sick, and lead the blind.
Just and holy is thy name,
I am all unrighteousness;
False and full of sin I am,
thou art full of truth and grace.**

Scripture

He heals the brokenhearted and bandages their wounds (Psalm 147:3).

Meditation

If you could have anything in the world, what would you choose?

We should choose Jesus. He should be all we want. Why? Because if we have Him, we have everything. He picks us up when we fall. He cheers us when our hearts are broken. He heals our bodies and restores our souls. He takes away all our sin, even when we are unrighteous.

We find everything in Jesus and more. More than we can imagine. In a world full of lies and deception, He is truth. Yet we find it hard to be content with Jesus alone. We are deceived by the four-letter words we constantly hear—"More! More! More!"

We must remind ourselves that all we want and need is in Him.

Stanza Four

**Plenteous grace with thee is found,
grace to cover all my sin;
let the healing streams abound,
make and keep me pure within.
Thou of life the fountain art:
freely let me take of thee,
spring thou up within my heart,
rise to all eternity.**

Scripture

For from his fullness we have all received, grace upon grace (John 1:16 ESV).

Meditation

It is sometimes harder to receive than to give. When we give, we are the generous ones, sharing our bounty with others. When we receive we are powerless and frail. No one wants to be the recipient of charity if they can help it.

But when it comes to God, we all are needy. We cannot be what we want to be without His help. And through Jesus, the one who loves us, the Lord freely gives beyond measure.

So we ask for the charity of God that cost Him His Son, but costs us nothing. Grace to cover all our sins. Grace that springs up in our hearts like a life-giving fountain. Grace that makes us pure within. Grace layered upon more grace.

For Reflection

1. When were times you felt like flying to Jesus for refuge? What shelter did He give you?
2. Is Jesus really all that you want? How do your other desires connect with your desire for Him?

3. When do you feel that you especially need grace from Jesus?

Live the Hymn

1. Take a few minutes today to meditate on all the ways that Jesus shows you His love.
2. In a specific act, show the grace of Jesus to someone today.

Prayer

Jesus, hide us in your love this day.

Day Eight:
Come, Holy Spirit, From on High (I)

STANZA ONE

Come, Holy Spirit, from on high,
Baptizer of our spirits thou!
The sacramental seal apply,
And witness with the water now.

SCRIPTURE

One day when the crowds were being baptized, Jesus himself was baptized. As he was praying, the heavens opened, and the Holy Spirit, in bodily form, descended on him like a dove. And a voice from heaven said, "You are my dearly loved Son, and you bring me great joy" (Luke 3:21-22).

MEDITATION

When Jesus was baptized, the heavens opened, the Spirit descended on Him, and the voice of God proclaimed that He was the beloved child.

The same thing happened at our baptisms, although we may not have realized it at the time. The heavens opened. There was no longer a barrier between us and God. The Spirit came upon us, although we may not have seen it in bodily form. And God spoke to each of us, saying that He was pleased with us as His dearly loved child.

Something supernatural happened at our baptism.

Stanza Two

Exert thy energy divine,
And sprinkle the atoning blood;
May Father, Son, and Spirit join
To seal this child, a child of God

Scripture

And since we have a great High Priest who rules over God's house, let us go right into the presence of God with sincere hearts fully trusting him. For our guilty consciences have been sprinkled with Christ's blood to make us clean, and our bodies have been washed with pure water (Hebrews 10:21-22).

Meditation

The first stanza of this hymn spoke of the sacramental seal of baptism. A sacrament is a ceremony that transmits the grace of God. Baptism is not an empty human ritual. God is the one acting in baptism, sprinkling us with the atoning blood of Jesus and placing His seal of approval on us.

God the Father calls us His children in baptism. Jesus the Son cleanses our consciences by His blood. The Holy Spirit comes on us to seal us and make us holy. In baptism, we participate in the very life of the Trinity.

Stanza Three

Come Holy Ghost, our hearts inspire,
let us thine influence prove;
source of the old prophetic fire,
fountain of life and love.

Scripture

A spiritual gift is given to each of us so we can help each other (1 Corinthians 12:7).

Meditation

Wesley uses the King James language of "Holy Ghost." We could take that to mean the Holy Spirit is ghostly and thus unreal, or we may see the Spirit as a mere insubstantial influence.

But the Bible speaks of the actions of the Spirit the same way it speak of God's actions.

Christians confess that the Spirit is a person of the Three-Fold God, the Trinity or Godhood.

The influence of the Spirit on our hearts is personal. He inspires our hearts. He brings the fiery word of God. He springs forth the water of life. He shows the love of God. We are infinitely poorer if we neglect the powerful gifts of the Spirit. That's why you can find mention of the Holy Spirit on almost every page of the New Testament.

But the gifts of the Spirit are not just for our own enjoyment; He gives those gifts so we can help others.

For Reflection

1. What did the Holy Spirit do at your baptism?
2. How is baptism a participation in the life of the Trinity?
3. What gift has the Holy Spirit given you?

Live the Hymn

1. Pray for a deeper experience of the Holy Spirit.
2. Use the gifts that the Spirit has given you to bless someone today.

Prayer

Holy Spirit, pour out your gifts into our hearts today, so we may bless others.

Day Nine:
Come, Holy Spirit, From on High (II).

STANZA FOUR

**Come, Holy Ghost, for, moved by thee,
thy prophets wrote and spoke:
unlock the truth, thyself the key,
unseal the sacred book.**

SCRIPTURE

But people who aren't spiritual can't receive these truths from God's Spirit. It all sounds foolish to them and they can't understand it, for only those who are spiritual can understand what the Spirit means (1 Corinthians 2:14).

MEDITATION

The Bible is like other books. It is written in ordinary human languages. It requires effort for us to read and understand it. There is no substitute for diligent Bible study.

The Bible is not like other books. God inspired it through the Holy Spirit. What is more, the Spirit works in us to open our hearts to the living and active word of God. So we carefully study the Bible. At the same time, we rely on the Spirit to show us what God wants us to understand, to obey, to do, and to be.

The Bible often uses the word "meditation" for this joining of our mind and the mind of the Spirit.

Stanza Five

**Expand thy wings, celestial Dove,
brood o'er our nature's night;
on our disordered spirits move,
and let there now be light.**

Scripture

The earth was formless and empty, and darkness covered the deep waters. And the Spirit of God was hovering over the surface of the waters (Genesis 1:2).

Meditation

"Creative" is an overused word. Almost everyone and everything is creative nowadays, but the Holy Spirit had a role in the creation of all things. He brooded or hovered over the waters before creation. The picture here is of a bird sitting on eggs or fluttering over its young in the nest

That same creative Spirit, the Holy Dove, broods over our nature, giving new birth to us (John 3:5-8). The Spirit gives direction to our disordered spirits and brings light to our darkness.

The call to us is not to direct our lives through our own creativity, but to submit to the Creative Voice who first said, "Let there be light," and humble ourselves under the Creative Hand that formed humans from the dust.

Stanza Six

**God, through himself, we then shall know,
if thou within us shine;**

**and sound, with all thy saints below,
the depths of love divine.**

Scripture

But it was to us that God revealed these things by his Spirit. For his Spirit searches out everything and shows us God's deep secrets (1 Corinthians 2:10).

Meditation

I have spent my whole life talking about what I do not know. I am not alone. We all talk of God. But who can fathom the Infinite and Almighty Spirit who rules all things? How can we describe God? How can we know anything about the Lord?

We can only know what He wants us to know. We can only speak of what He has revealed to us. God unveils Himself, showing His glory in the beauty of nature. God speaks through prophets. He shows himself in the words of the Bible.

It is the Spirit who reveals God to us in Scripture, tradition, experience, and reason. And what do we know of God through these revelations? We know that God is love. On our own, we never would have discovered the depth of God's love.

For Reflection

1. How is the Bible both like and unlike other books?
2. How does the Spirit help us understand the word of God?
3. What are some ways the Spirit reveals God?

Live the Hymn

1. Meditate on the word of God today.
2. Let the Spirit inspire creativity in you.

Prayer

Spirit, open the ears of our hearts so we may hear the God of love speak.

Day Ten:
Forth in Your Name

STANZA ONE

**Forth in your name, O Lord, I go,
my daily labor to pursue,
determined only you to know
in all I think or speak or do.**

SCRIPTURE

Work willingly at whatever you do, as though you were working for the Lord rather than for people. Remember that the Lord will give you an inheritance as your reward, and that the Master you are serving is Christ (Colossians 3:23-24).

MEDITATION

Is God doing all His work in us through the Holy Spirit? Or are we to work as hard as we can to please the Lord?

The clear answer is "Yes" to both questions. Relying on the power of the Spirit within us takes away the pressure to always do things right by our own efforts. Yet Jesus calls us to make every effort to love God and love our neighbors.

This call to dedicated service is a call to freedom. We do not have to be clever enough or good enough or powerful enough to solve all the world's problems. We only need to do our daily tasks for the Lord. He will take care of His world.

Stanza Two

**The task your wisdom has assigned,
O let me cheerfully fulfill;
in all my works your presence find,
and prove your good and perfect will.**

Scripture

Don't copy the behavior and customs of this world, but let God transform you into a new person by changing the way you think. Then you will learn to know God's will for you, which is good and pleasing and perfect (Romans 12:2).

Meditation

"What is God's plan for my life?"

I taught in a Christian college for years. I had many students who were obsessed with the question of God's will for their lives Some of them spent so much time worrying about God's future plans for them that they neglected their studies.

It's not only college students who do this. Many conscientious Christians wonder what the will of God is for their lives. But we learn God's perfect will for us by doing the tasks He has assigned to us today.

Stanza Three

**May I find you at my right hand;
your eyes see truly what I do.
I labor on at your command
And offer all my works to you.**

Scripture

"I have set the Lord always before me; because he is at my right hand, I shall not be shaken" (Psalm 16:8 ESV).

Meditation

The right hand of God is the place where Jesus is seated (Mark 16:19. Hebrews 1:3-4, 10:12-13, 12:1-2, Ephesians 1:15-23). This means Jesus has all power, reigning with God the Father.

This hymn and Bible verse says that the Lord is on our right hand. That does not mean we are equal or superior to God. It does mean that God—Father, Son, and Spirit—are always near to help us. We sometimes use the phrase, "my right-hand man" to refer to the person (male or female) on whom we depend the most.

If we see the Lord as our right-hand man (meaning no disrespect), it changes how we do the mundane jobs that seem so insignificant.

Stanza Four

**Give me to bear your easy yoke
and ev'ry moment watch and pray
and still to things eternal look,
and hasten to your glorious day.**

Scripture

But stay awake at all times, praying that you may have strength to escape all these things that are going to take place, and to stand before the Son of Man (Luke 21:36).

Meditation

Many chores are a burden because they are so daily. Cleaning, cooking, and the twice-a-day commute—these are not too hard for us, but they never end. Tomorrow we will have to do them again.

Those tasks are easier with Jesus pulling the plow beside us. He takes on our yoke and makes it easy. But even in the daily jobs, Jesus calls us to be alert to His Presence now and His coming return. We face our duties each day with an eye toward eternity. We watch and pray.

Watching does not mean we keep the Second Coming in our minds at all times. I'm not sure that is possible. It does mean that we place each day in the hands of God, and we pray that Jesus comes soon.

Stanza Five

**For you I joyously employ
whate'er you in grace have giv'n:
I run my daily course with joy
and closely walk with you to heav'n.**

Scripture

By this we may know that we are in him: whoever says he abides in him ought to walk in the same way in which he walked (1 John 2:6 ESV).

Meditation

We all had to learn to walk. We do it without thinking now, but at one point it took great concentration. Perhaps, after an illness, you've had to learn to walk again.

We walk to get places, but many of us walk for exercise. That walking takes planning and discipline. We walk a certain amount every day, whether we feel like it or not.

The Bible often compares our life in Christ to a walk. We must learn to walk with Jesus. The first steps are often frightening. We fall repeatedly. But Jesus is there, holding our hand, and happy to be walking with us. Walking daily with the Lord takes practice. It requires discipline. We do it when we do not especially feel like it.

But there is great joy in that walk.

For Reflection

1. What part does the Holy Spirit play in our actions? What part do we play?
2. What does it mean to watch for Jesus to come?
3. What does it take to walk with Jesus?

Live the Hymn

1. Imagine that Jesus is right beside you as you work for Him today.
2. Imagine that Jesus is with you in every step you take.

Prayer

Lord Jesus, grant us the strength to walk with you and work for you this day.

Day Eleven:
Christ, Whose Glory Fills the Skies

Stanza One

Christ, whose glory fills the skies,
Christ, the true and only Light,
Sun of righteousness, arise,
triumph o'er the shade of night;
Day-spring from on high, be near;
Day-star, in my heart appear.

Scripture

Because of that experience, we have even greater confidence in the message proclaimed by the prophets. You must pay close attention to what they wrote, for their words are like a lamp shining in a dark place—until the Day dawns, and Christ the Morning Star shines in your hearts (2 Peter 1:19).

Meditation

Why do we study the Bible? For some of us, Bible study is a good habit we have had for years. For others of us, it is a chore, a mere duty. We know we should meditate on the Bible, but we can't seem to find the time. But when we walk into a dark room, we always find time to turn on the lights. We don't even think about it because we need to see where we are going.

In the same way, the Scriptures, the message of the prophets that point to Jesus, give light to us in the dark room of life. That's why we pay close attention to what they wrote.

Stanza Two

Dark and cheerless is the morn
unaccompanied by Thee;
joyless is the day's return,
till Thy mercy's beams I see,
till they inward light impart,
glad my eyes, and warm my heart.

Scripture

The light shines in the darkness, and the darkness can never extinguish it (John 1:5).

Meditation

After days of gloom, we long for the sun. Stumbling in the dark, we ache for the light. In the agony of searching for direction for our lives, we hunger for the dawn of understanding.

Christ is our light. His glory is like the sun. He shines in the darkness. He is the Morning Star that announces the dawn. In the murkiest shadows of pain, loss, and bewilderment, Jesus pours His brilliance into our hearts. We need only to open the eyes of our hearts to see the way He illuminates. And no matter how dark our world looks, we know that the darkness can never extinguish the light of Jesus. This is not the optimism of "look on the sunny side of life," but is the sure hope in the warming mercy of God,

Stanza Three

Visit then this soul of mine,
pierce the gloom of sin and grief;
fill me, radiancy divine,

**scatter all my unbelief;
more and more Thyself display,
shining to the perfect day.**

Scripture

For God, who said, "Let there be light in the darkness," has made this light shine in our hearts so we could know the glory of God that is seen in the face of Jesus Christ (2 Corinthians 4:6).

Meditation

Are you a person of light or a person of darkness? When people meet you, do they see you as gloomy? Or do you light up a room when you enter?

This is not a question of personalities. An introvert can be light or darkness as well as an extrovert can. It is not a matter of circumstances. We can be light when tragedy strikes and be dark when everything is wonderful. It is not even a matter of willpower. Being light is more than putting on a happy face.

Our light comes from within, from the glorious face of Jesus shining in our hearts. The more Jesus fills us, the more light we shine on others.

For Reflection

1. How does the Bible bring light into our lives?
2. How is biblical hope different from looking on the bright side?
3. Do people see you as one who lights the way for them?

Live the Hymn

1. Let the words of the Bible give light to you today.
2. Find someone who is having a dark day. Shine some light on them.

Prayer

Glorious Lord Jesus, radiate from our hearts today.

Day Twelve:
O For a Heart to Praise my God

STANZA ONE

O for a heart to praise my God,
a heart from sin set free;
a heart that's sprinkled with the blood
so freely shed for me:

SCRIPTURE

Let us draw near with a true heart in full assurance of faith, with our hearts sprinkled clean from an evil conscience and our bodies washed with pure water (Hebrews 10:22, ESV).

MEDITATION

The Bible speaks of the heart as the center of our being. The heart is not just the source of our emotions but also of our thinking, our will, and our actions.

What separates us from God? Perhaps our emotions. We don't always feel close to God. But mainly it is our actions that detach us from the will of God.

What reunites us to God? How can we be sure that we are right with Him? That assurance comes from a heart washed clean by the blood of Jesus, given on the cross. Even when we might not feel close to God, faith makes us certain that He has forgiven us and made us pure in His sight. How do our hearts respond to that cleansing?

They praise our God.

Stanza Two

A heart resigned, submissive, meek,
my great Redeemer's throne;
where only Christ is heard to speak,
where Jesus reigns alone:

Scripture

And let the peace that comes from Christ rule in your hearts. For as members of one body you are called to live in peace. And always be thankful (Colossians 3:15).

Meditation

What rules your life?

The clock rules. Our jobs control us. The obligations of family constrain us. For some, money and the making of it rules.

What we want is to rule our own lives. We want control over our jobs, our family, and our finances. There are many books and programs that promise us that mastery.

What if Jesus really ruled our lives? What if we placed family, job, money, and our pursuit of happiness completely under His power? What would that look like?

Peace. It would look like peace. Perhaps we should try it today.

Stanza Three

A humble, lowly, contrite heart,
believing, true, and clean,
which neither life nor death can part
from him that dwells within:

SCRIPTURE

The sacrifices of God are a broken spirit; a broken and contrite heart, O God, you will not despise (Psalm 51:17, ESV).

MEDITATION

A broken heart. No one wants their heart broken, but we've all felt that deep pain. Rejected by one we love, we don't know if we will ever be the same.

The Bible speaks of a different kind of broken heart. When we see how we have treated the God who loves us, our hearts break. They break because we know that our rejection of God's love breaks His heart. Out of that broken heart, Jesus gave his life for us while we were still sinners (Romans 5:8).

So our hearts are now broken in a good way, broken so that the love of God through Christ can enter our humbled hearts, and broken so that we can share the good news of God's love for all those who are broken.

STANZA FOUR

**A heart in every thought renewed,
and full of love divine;
perfect and right and pure and good —
a copy, Lord, of thine.**

SCRIPTURE

Create in me a clean heart, O God. Renew a loyal spirit within me (Psalm 51:10).

MEDITATION

According to tradition, David wrote Psalm 51 after Nathan the prophet rebuked him for adultery with Bathsheba and the murder of her husband Uriah. Few of us have committed adultery and murder, but like David, we have hurt others in shameful ways. If those around us do not know our sins, the Lord knows. He might even send a friend to confront us, as he sent Nathan to David.

When we see our sins, we can react in several ways. "I didn't mean to." "It's not my fault." "Others have done worse." David reacts with honesty. "I have sinned." If we also admit our guilt, we can cry out for the clean heart God promises, a heart that is perfect and right and pure and good. God will give us His heart, His Holy Spirit, a heart full of His love.

Stanza Five

**Thy nature, gracious Lord, impart,
come quickly from above;
write thy new name upon my heart,
thy new best name of Love.**

Scripture

And because of his glory and excellence, he has given us great and precious promises. These are the promises that enable you to share his divine nature and escape the world's corruption caused by human desires (2 Peter 1:4).

Meditation

It seems too much to imagine that God would give us His heart. How can we love as God loves? His love is infinite. He is love itself. How can we measure up to that?

Yet that is what God promises. He promises forgiveness and relationship with Him so we may participate in God's very nature. Jesus became human so that we might be divine.

This is completely different from Adam and Eve wanting to be like God when tempted by the serpent. They wanted to like God in their own way. Jesus, the new Adam, begins a new humanity in the image of God.

Jesus writes the Name of God on our hearts through the Holy Spirit. He gives us the name of Love.

For Reflection

1. What does "heart" mean in the Bible?
2. How can a broken heart be a good thing?
3. What does it mean to share in God's nature?

Live the Hymn

1. When you pray today, fall face down before the Lord with a heart broken by sin. Accept his complete cleansing of your heart.
2. Listen from your heart to what Jesus is saying to you.

Prayer

Freed from sin, we give you heartfelt praise, our God!

Day Thirteen:
Jesus, Thine All-Victorious Love

STANZA ONE

Jesus, thine all-victorious love
shed in my heart abroad;
then shall my feet no longer rove,
rooted and fixed in God.

SCRIPTURE

Then Christ will make his home in your hearts as you trust in him. Your roots will grow down into God's love and keep you strong (Ephesians 3:17).

MEDITATION

I don't know much about gardening. I like to plant flowers and trees in our yard, but many of them do not survive. What I do know is that having deep roots makes for a healthy plant. Deep roots ground trees in a storm. Deep roots provide nourishment even in a drought.

We used to hear much about church growth. Much of that talk was about how to increase the numbers of people who came to church. But Christians and churches are like plants; to grow they must have deep roots. We need to focus more on growing deeper into the love of God.

That deep growth is a gift of God. He plants. He waters. He is the sun that nourishes us. What we must do is to stay rooted in Him instead of drifting and roving. We do that through prayer, Bible study, and service.

STANZA TWO

**O that in me the sacred fire
might now begin to glow;
burn up the dross of base desire
and make the mountains flow!**

SCRIPTURE

"John answered their questions by saying, 'I baptize you with water; but someone is coming soon who is greater than I am—so much greater that I'm not even worthy to be his slave and untie the straps of his sandals. He will baptize you with the Holy Spirit and with fire'" (Luke 3:16).

MEDITATION

We move from the growth of trees to the fire that destroys trees. As I write this, wildfires are burning thousands of acres and hundreds of homes. It is hard to imagine the destructive force of such fires.

We are rightly afraid of fire. But what would we do without fire? Fire in different forms warms our houses, heats our meals, and provides light for our cities.

God is a consuming fire (Deuteronomy 4:24 and Hebrews 12:29). Jesus came to baptize with fire. Should the fire of God frighten us? Yes, in the same way we are cautious around all fires. We dare not toy with God. He wants only to warm us in His love.

STANZA THREE

**O that it now from heaven might fall
and all my sins consume!
Come, Holy Ghost, for thee I call,**

Spirit of burning, come!

SCRIPTURE

This is why I remind you to fan into flames the spiritual gift God gave you when I laid my hands on you. For God has not given us a spirit of fear and timidity, but of power, love, and self-discipline (2 Timothy 1:6-7).

MEDITATION

What does the fire of God consume? The Lord does not want to burn His people. What He desires is for His fire to completely burn away our sin. The fire of the Holy Spirit consumes all that would turn us against God, leaving only obedient and holy lives.

When that fire of the Lord burns within us, we have the intensity of the Spirit's flame. We burn not with anger or hatred toward others, but with the frightening love of Jesus. That firestorm in our hearts gives us the power for sacrificial service. It blazes with love, even for our enemies. It disciplines us so we might deny our desires in order to provide for others.

Through the Spirit, the Lord burns away our old self to give birth to the new self in His image.

STANZA FOUR

**Refining fire, go through my heart,
illuminate my soul;
scatter thy life through every part
and sanctify the whole.**

SCRIPTURE

I will bring that group through the fire and make them pure. I will refine them like silver and purify them like gold. They will call on my name, and I will answer them. I will say, "These are my people," and they will say, "The Lord is our God" (Zechariah 13:9).

MEDITATION

Why do Christians suffer?

There are many good answers to that question. Here is one: We suffer because the Lord is refining us. Perhaps you've been to a forge and watched those who work with molten metal. The heat is unbearable. Those who work there always chance burns on their bodies.

Burns hurt. Why would a loving God burn His people? Because He is refining us, making sure that every part of us is pure. It is so hard at times to accept that burning love. We would rather be comfortable. But even in the worst of torment, when our hearts ache and throb, we trust the sanctifying warmth of God's love.

FOR REFLECTION

1. What are some ways you can grow deeper into God's love?
2. How is God like a fire? Is that a good thing or a bad thing?
3. Why is it sometimes painful to follow Jesus?

LIVE THE HYMN

1. Think of yourself today as on fire for Jesus.
2. Give your pain up to God as part of His effort to refine you.

PRAYER

Spirit of burning, enflame our hearts and minds.

Day Fourteen:
Soldiers of Christ, Arise (I)

STANZA ONE

**Soldiers of Christ, arise,
and put your armor on,
strong in the strength which God supplies
thro' His eternal Son;**

SCRIPTURE

Put on all of God's armor so that you will be able to stand firm against all strategies of the devil (Ephesians 6:11).

MEDITATION

Jesus is the Prince of Peace. He is the gentle Savior who caries our burdens. He died to make us right with God, taking all our sins away. He gives us His Holy Spirit. All is by His grace. It is free. By faith we have absolute assurance of our salvation.

It all sounds so easy! So why is there so much talk of fighting and war in the Bible? Because following Jesus is a struggle. There are enemies out there and enemies inside us. To be clear, our fight is not a violent battle against national or personal enemies. "For we are not fighting against flesh-and-blood enemies, but against evil rulers and authorities of the unseen world, against mighty powers in this dark world, and against evil spirits in the heavenly places" (Ephesians 6:12).

It is a battle where we need armor against such powerful enemies.

Stanza Two

**strong in the Lord of hosts
and in His mighty pow'r,
who in the strength of Jesus trusts
is more than conqueror.**

Scripture

No, in all these things we are more than conquerors through him who loved us (Romans 8:37, ESV).

Meditation

We fight against supernatural and cosmic forces of evil. It sounds like one of those superhero comics or films. Much of the time we do not take evil seriously enough. We know people make mistakes and bad choices, but we would not call that "evil."

But real evil exists. It's hard to make sense of what we see in the news—mass shootings, gruesome murders, and genocide—without thinking there are evil forces at play.

Weak as we are, how can we fight such evil? By relying on one stronger than the greatest superhero. He is the Lord of Hosts, the commander of heaven's army. He is the Conquering Lamb, whose blood shed on the cross defeats all enemies. He is the ultimate power, the Holy Spirit, whose fire burns away all evil. He triumphs through us!

Stanza Three

**Stand then in His great might,
with all His strength endued,
and take, to aid you in the fight,**

the panoply of God.

SCRIPTURE

Therefore, my brothers, whom I love and long for, my joy and crown, stand firm thus in the Lord, my beloved (Philippians 4:1, ESV).

MEDITATION

What does it take to win this great conflict against evil? We must stand firm (Ephesians 6:11, 13, 14). We stand our ground no matter what Satan throws against us. We never give up. But this perseverance comes not from our own strength, but from the gifts that God gives us for battle—God's own armor. Isaiah tells how God could not find justice on the earth, so he stepped in to fight for it. The Lord put on "righteousness as his body armor and placed the helmet of salvation on his head" (Isaiah 59:17).

God shares His array of armor with us—His array of the belt of truth, the body armor of salvation, the shoes of good news, the shield of faith, the helmet of salvation, and the sword of the Spirit—so we might win the battle through His strength.

FOR REFLECTION

1. How is being a Christian like fighting a battle?
2. Who is our enemy?
3. What does it take to never back down from the battle Jesus calls us to fight?

LIVE THE HYMN

1. Use prayer to depend on the power of Jesus for your fight today.
2. Take some time to meditate on each of the parts of the armor of God.

PRAYER

As we wrestle and fight and pray, Jesus make us fight your way.

Day Fifteen:
Soldiers of Christ, Arise (II)

STANZA FOUR

**From strength to strength go on,
wrestle and fight and pray;
tread all the pow'rs of darkness down
and win the well-fought day.**

SCRIPTURE

We use God's mighty weapons, not worldly weapons, to knock down the strongholds of human reasoning and to destroy false arguments. We destroy every proud obstacle that keeps people from knowing God. We capture their rebellious thoughts and teach them to obey Christ (2 Corinthians 10:4-5).

MEDITATION

We might think that winning is everything in the fight against evil, but we must win with the right weapons.

Yet Christians easily grab for the "worldly weapons" to fight their battles. Violence, political power, money, superior numbers, image, shame, manipulation, deceptive talk, and alternative facts are just some of the ways Christians take up arms against others. We often demonize our enemies instead of seeing them as humans made in God's image.

If we fight like Jesus, we win only through sacrificial love.

Stanza Five

**Leave no unguarded place,
no weakness of the soul;
take every virtue, every grace,
and fortify the whole.**

Scripture

Therefore, put on every piece of God's armor so you will be able to resist the enemy in the time of evil. Then after the battle you will still be standing firm (Ephesians 6:13).

Meditation

There is disagreement about the precise meaning of each of these pieces of armor, but the point is clear. We must stand firm in the battle. What is missed in many translations is that the command to put on the pieces of armor is plural. That is, He says "Y'all" or "You guys" put on the armor. We do not stand alone. We are a band of brothers and sisters together in combat against evil.

Most importantly, God is fighting with us and through us. We tap into His infinite strength through prayer. "Pray in the Spirit at all times and on every occasion. Stay alert and be persistent in your prayers for all believers everywhere" (Ephesians 6:18). Prayer in the Spirit means we rely on His power, not our own.

Stanza Six

**That, having all things done
and all your conflicts past,
ye may o'ercome thro' Christ alone
and stand complete at last.**

Scripture

"I have told you all this so that you may have peace in me. Here on earth you will have many trials and sorrows. But take heart, because I have overcome the world" (John 16:33).

Meditation

When we watch or read the news, it looks like evil has triumphed. Satan, demons, corrupt governments, war, poverty, hunger, and crime are too rampant for powerless people like us to stand against them. We react with fear and hopelessness until we recall who is on our side. He is the Lord Almighty. He is the commander of the heavenly army and He invites us to join up.

Christ wants you!

When we enlist in His army, we join veterans throughout the ages who have triumphed through faith. We join brothers and sisters throughout the world who are standing firm in spite of opposition. We join the band of heavenly angels. We are not afraid, because we have put on the armor and followed our general into battle. This may sound too grand for our daily battles with sin and wrongdoing, but in those everyday struggles, we stand complete with Jesus.

For Reflection

1. What are some ways we should not use to fight evil?
2. Who fights with us against evil?
3. How can we be certain that we will win the battle?

Live the Hymn

1. As you go about your day, view yourself in a constant fight against all that is unholy.
2. Spend some time recalling the victories you have attained through Jesus.

Prayer

Holy Spirit, join us together in the fight against the enemy. Make us stand firm.

Day Sixteen:
Let Earth and Heaven Agree

Stanza One

Let earth and Heaven agree,
Angels and men be joined,
To celebrate with me
The Saviour of mankind;
To adore the all-atoning Lamb,
And bless the sound of Jesus' name.

Scripture

Christ suffered for our sins once for all time. He never sinned, but he died for sinners to bring you safely home to God. He suffered physical death, but he was raised to life in the Spirit (1 Peter 3:18).

Meditation

The name of Jesus is powerful. We celebrate it as the name of the one who atones for our sins and saves all humanity. But the name itself is not magical. Some Jewish exorcists in Ephesus try to use the name of Jesus to cast out a demon. The demon says it knows Jesus but not them. The evil spirit then turns its violence on them (Acts 19:13-16).

If we use the name of Jesus, then we must adore and celebrate it.

Stanza Two

**Jesus, transporting sound,
The joy of earth and Heaven;
No other help is found,
No other name is given
By which we can salvation have;
But Jesus came the world to save.**

Scripture

There is salvation in no one else! God has given no other name under heaven by which we must be saved (Acts 4:12).

Meditation

This "no other name" verse has caused great discussion. Does it mean that those who have never heard of Jesus are eternally lost? Or does it mean that even those who do not know of Jesus will be saved in His name?

I don't have an easy answer to the question, but the point of these words is not to decide who is included or excluded in salvation. Peter and John had healed a lame man at the temple gate. For this offense, the council of Jewish leaders demands what authority have for this act. "By what power, or in whose name, have you done this?" That's when the two disciples say, "by the powerful name of Jesus Christ the Nazarene."

The point is that Jesus saves!

Stanza Three

His name the sinner hears,
And is from sin set free;
'Tis music in his ears,
'Tis life and victory!
New songs do now his lips employ,
And dances his glad heart for joy.

Scripture

You have turned my mourning into joyful dancing. You have taken away my clothes of mourning and clothed me with joy (Psalm 30:11).

Meditation

I was raised in a church that frowned on dancing. No doubt there are some dances that might lead you away from God.

But God's people often dance for joy because of what He has done for them. After the Lord delivers Israel through the Red Sea, the women dance and sing (Exodus 15:20). When David brings the Ark of the Covenant into Jerusalem, he leaps and dances (2 Samuel 6:16). When the Prodigal Son returns home, they celebrate with music and dancing (Luke 15:25).

When we hear the name of Jesus, we respond with song and dance. A healthy church dances more, not less.

Stanza Four

O unexampled love!
O all-redeeming grace!
How swiftly didst thou move

> To save a fallen race:
> What shall I do to make it known
> What thou for all mankind hast done?

SCRIPTURE

But my life is worth nothing to me unless I use it for finishing the work assigned me by the Lord Jesus—the work of telling others the Good News about the wonderful grace of God (Acts 20:24).

MEDITATION

"Gospel" means good news.

We love to share good news. "My daughter is getting married." "I got a raise at work." "The cancer is in remission." "I know where you can get a bargain." We are eager to share such news.

Yet we are sometimes hesitant to tell the best news of all—the news of the love and grace of Jesus.

We may shy away from telling others we are Christians because we're not sure how they will react. Perhaps they've been burned by those who turned the "gospel" into bad news, but if we sing and dance at the name of Jesus, we should tell His name to others.

STANZA FIVE

> O for a trumpet voice
> On all the world to call,
> To bid their hearts rejoice
> In him who died for all!
> For all my Lord was crucified,
> For all, for all my Saviour died.

Scripture

He died for everyone so that those who receive his new life will no longer live for themselves. Instead, they will live for Christ, who died and was raised for them (2 Corinthians 5:15).

Meditation

Did Jesus die only for the good, church-going people? The way some Christians act, that's what you might think, but the Bible often says that Jesus died for all. All means all. Everyone. Yes, even them.

Does that mean everyone will be saved? When I bring up this question to my Christian friends, they are quick to say that only the believing and obedient will be saved. Perhaps they are right. The Bible speaks that way in certain verses. But we dare not take joy or comfort in that fact.

Jesus died for all. God wants everyone to be saved. The Spirit moves wherever He wants. And if all are saved, wouldn't that be a glorious thing?

For Reflection

1. Why is Jesus the greatest name?
2. Is dancing a good thing or a bad thing?
3. How would you feel if God saved everyone?

Live the Hymn

1. Today dance a joyous dance before the Lord.
2. Share the good news of Jesus today by word and action.

Prayer

Jesus, may we joyfully celebrate your good news today.

Day Seventeen:
Weary of Wandering From my God

STANZA ONE

Weary of wandering from my God
And now made willing to return,
I hear, and bow me to the rod;
For thee, not without hope, I mourn.
I have an advocate above,
A friend before the throne of love.

SCRIPTURE

My dear children, I am writing this to you so that you will not sin. But if anyone does sin, we have an advocate who pleads our case before the Father. He is Jesus Christ, the one who is truly righteous (1 John 2:1).

MEDITATION

What happens when we stray from God, or when we do more than stray, when we deliberately turn from Jesus and hurt those we love? How do we react when our actions are so extraordinarily out of character for us?

We can reject our faith. We can blame others for our behavior. We can wallow in shame and guilt. We can even despair, thinking we can never change.

Or we can long to be right with God again. Out of that yearning, we can turn back to the one who pleads our case, Jesus our advocate who shares His righteousness with us.

Stanza Two

O Jesus, full of truth and grace,
More full of grace than I of sin,
Yet once again I seek thy face,
Open thine arms and take me in,
And freely my backslidings heal
And love the faithless sinner still.

Scripture

You have said, "Seek my face." My heart says to you, "Your face, Lord, do I seek" (Psalm 27:8 ESV).

Meditation

Have you ever wounded those you love so much that you wanted to hide from them? Perhaps you've been so mortified by your selfish actions that you could not show your face in church or anywhere in public.

There is One whose face we dare not try to hide from. Nothing is hidden from His sight. Yet the astounding truth is, He loves us even when we feel like avoiding Him at all costs. If we turn to Him we will find His face is not scowling in anger, but radiant with compassion.

Like the father in the story of the Prodigal Son (Luke 15:11-32), Jesus waits for us to return, opening His arms to the faithless sinner who is His beloved child.

Stanza Three

Thou knowest the way to bring me back,
My fallen spirit to restore;
O for thy truth and mercy's sake
Forgive, and bid me sin no more!
The ruins of my soul repair
And make my heart a house of prayer.

Scripture

You will seek me and find me, when you seek me with all your heart (Jeremiah 29:13 ESV).

Meditation

Forgiveness from Jesus wipes the slate clean. Our sins no longer count. God remembers them no more.

The redemption we have in Jesus does much more than that. It restores us. You've likely seen a master craftsman restore an old, beat-up piece of furniture until it looked like new. That's what Jesus does for us when we turn to Him. He refurbishes the very center of our being—what the Bible calls the heart—making it a place of prayer.

Out of gratitude for that extreme makeover, we continue to seek the face of God. In prayer and in service to others we give praise to the one who has made us new. We ask the Carpenter of Nazareth to remake us in His image each day.

For Reflection

1. What might make us weary from wandering from God?
2. Have you ever tried to hide from God? Why?
3. When have you experienced the restoration that Jesus promises?

Live the Hymn

1. Freely admit your wandering from God.
2. Instead of trying to hide from God, pray today with your face lifted toward heaven and your eyes wide open.

Prayer

Great Artisan of our lives, retore our fallen spirits this day!

Day Eighteen:
Jesus, My Truth, My Way

STANZA ONE

Jesus, my truth, my way,
My sure, unerring light,
On thee my feeble steps I stay,
Which thou wilt guide aright.

SCRIPTURE

Jesus told him, "I am the way, the truth, and the life. No one can come to the Father except through me" (John 14:6).

MEDITATION

Have you ever been lost in the woods? I have, and it was a harrowing experience. I thought I knew the way back to where I was staying, but somehow I lost the path. I was alone. The only light I had was from my phone. Then I heard the voices of other people. Following those voices, I found the trail to safety.

We sometimes feel lost in the familiar actions of our day. We go through the motions of life but don't know what it's all about. What we need is a clear voice to follow. What we need is a brighter light to see the way. What we need is a reliable signpost.

Jesus is all that. He is the truth that points the way. He is the sure light. He is the guide we can trust. All He asks is that we put one foot in front of the other and follow Him.

Stanza Two

**My wisdom and my guide,
My Counsellor thou art;
O never let me leave thy side,
Or from thy paths depart!**

Scripture

When the Spirit of truth comes, he will guide you into all truth. He will not speak on his own but will tell you what he has heard. He will tell you about the future. He will bring me glory by telling you whatever he receives from me (John 16:13-14).

Meditation

There are times when we all could use some good advice. We need someone with experience who can show us how something is done or guide us through a tough decision.

We need a wise counselor; not so much a trained psychologist (although they also have their place), but a reliable friend. Jesus is that Counselor. He guides us though the Bible. He shows us the way through the assistance from fellow Christians. He even speaks to our hearts in a gentle whisper.

We must make the effort to listen. And when we hear His wise advice, we must be willing to follow it, even when it leads down difficult paths, even when we can barely hear His whisper, but we know He is there.

Stanza Three

**Teach me the happy art
In all things to depend
On thee; O never, Lord, depart,**

But love me to the end!

SCRIPTURE

Before the Passover celebration, Jesus knew that his hour had come to leave this world and return to his Father. He had loved his disciples during his ministry on earth, and now he loved them to the very end (John 13:1).

MEDITATION

I have not heard from some of those who were my closest friends for years, which means our friendships did not last. At one point I would have called them my closest friends, but we moved to other places, lost touch, and grew apart.

The most precious relationships are those that last.

Jesus promises never to leave us. Even when He was physically leaving the disciples through His death, resurrection, and ascension, He promised to always be with them. He gave His Holy Spirit to those who believe so we might have Jesus with us always. He loves us to the end of our lives and the end of all things. He will love us in the new heaven and earth.

STANZA FOUR

Let me thy witness live,
When sin is all destroyed;
And then my spotless soul receive,
And take me home to God.

SCRIPTURE

And now the prize awaits me—the crown of righteousness, which the Lord, the righteous Judge, will give me on the day of his return. And the prize is not just for me but for all who eagerly look forward to his appearing (2 Timothy 4:8).

Meditation

"You can't go home again."

So says the title of the novel by Thomas Wolfe. There's some truth in that statement. Once you leave your parents' home, even when you visit, it is not the same. You have grown. They've changed. Nothing remains the same.

We long to go back to the old homeplace, to a simpler time when our family sheltered and cherished us. We want to feel our mother's embrace and see our father's smile. We don't feel quite at home anywhere anymore.

But our true home is waiting.

For Reflection

1. What are the ways that Jesus guides us?
2. Why does Jesus promise to never leave us?
3. What comes to mind when you think of home?

Live the Hymn

1. Try to remember the relief you felt the last time you found the right directions after being lost. Feel that same relief at how Jesus has guided you. Let Him guide you today.
2. Long for your true home with God today.

Prayer

Jesus, you are the Way. Give us strength to follow.

Day Nineteen:
All Praise to our Redeeming Lord (I)

STANZA ONE

All praise to our redeeming Lord,
who joins us by his grace,
and bids us, each to each restored,
together seek his face.

SCRIPTURE

For where two or three gather together as my followers, I am there among them (Matthew 18:20).

MEDITATION

"I don't really need the church to feel close to God."

I hear that often. We live in the age of "me and Jesus" Christianity. If others want to come along, fine, but it's all about me and Jesus.

The Bible does not talk much about you and Jesus. Most of the time, the Bible addresses "y'all" or "you guys" and Jesus. When we hear Jesus say, "Follow me," and we go with Him, we always join others on the journey. God the Father through Jesus and the Spirit joins us together with other believers by His grace. Church is not optional. We seek the Lord together, and when we walk the path of trust together, Jesus promises to be with us. We never walk alone.

Stanza Two

He bids us build each other up;
and, gathered into one,
to our high calling's glorious hope
we hand in hand go on.

Scripture

So encourage each other and build each other up, just as you are already doing (1 Thessalonians 5:11).

Meditation

Do we build others up or tear them down?

I have spent much of my life being clever. Because I thought I was smarter than others, it was easy to find creative ways to put them down. We know how much it hurts when we face ridicule, so why do we belittle others? I guess we think it makes us look smarter or better if we make fun of them.

But what if we were walking down the same path hand-in-hand? Then we would not want others to stumble, for we would fall with them. What if the Lord judged us not as individuals but as a church? Then we would feel responsible for one another. Then we would build others up, not tear them down.

Stanza Three

The gift which he on one bestows,
we all delight to prove;
the grace through every vessel flows,
in purest streams of love.

Scripture

God has given each of you a gift from his great variety of spiritual gifts. Use them well to serve one another (1 Peter 4:10).

Meditation

If you have an IQ above 130 then you are gifted. Perhaps you were a gifted child or you have gifted children. If so, it is likely a point of pride. How ironic! If we are more intelligent than others (and everyone is more intelligent than others in some way) it is because God has given us that gift. How dare we think ourselves superior to others when we only receive God's grace, just as others do?

The Holy Spirit does not give us gifts so we might compare ourselves to others. God does not want us to be jealous of the gifts others have. Neither does He want us to be arrogant about our gifts. He gives, not so that we might feel gifted, but so we can serve others.

So let us worry less about what gift we have and concentrate more on how we can help those around us. We are graced to give.

For Reflection

1. Does one need the church to follow Jesus? Why or why not?
2. Why do we sometimes tear others down instead of building them up?
3. What gift has God given you that you can use to serve others?

Live the Hymn

1. Be intentional today in building others up, not tearing them down.
2. Use the gifts the Spirit has given you to help others.

Prayer

Jesus, keep us together as your people, walking together in love.

Day Twenty:
All Praise to our Redeeming Lord (II)

STANZA FOUR

**Ev'n now we think and speak the same,
and cordially agree;
concentered all, through Jesus' name,
in perfect harmony.**

SCRIPTURE

Make every effort to keep yourselves united in the Spirit, binding yourselves together with peace (Ephesians 4:3).

MEDITATION

"Love your neighbor as yourself."

No one objects to loving the neighbor, but what if your neighbor is wrong? What if this "neighbor" is a fellow Christian who disagrees strongly with you? How can we love our brothers and sisters who misunderstand the Bible? After studying with them, do we write them off as false Christians who will not accept the obvious truth? Or do we love them as full brothers and sisters in spite of their "error?"

We can think of other issues that divide Christians; some we think are important, even central to the faith. But agreement is not what unites us; it is the love of God in Christ. Even if our brothers and sisters are wrong, we leave their judgment to Christ. Even if we are wrong (and we have been before), we leave our judgment in the hands of a gracious Savior.

Stanza Five

**We all partake the joy of one,
the common peace we feel,
a peace to sensual minds unknown,
a joy unspeakable.**

Scripture

Rejoice with those who rejoice; mourn with those who mourn (Romans 12:15, NIV).

Meditation

If you got a message from your boss saying, "Because of your excellent work you are receiving a bonus of $10,000," how would you feel? How would you feel if you found out that everyone in your department got the bonus? Would you be happier, or would you be disappointed because you were not special? What if your best friend got the bonus, but you did not? Would you be as thrilled?

It is hard to share someone's joy if we have no reason to celebrate. In Christ we are all in this together, and another's blessedness is our own. This kind of peaceful participation in each other's lives makes no sense to those who are always out for #1. But we follow the one who came to serve rather than to be served, so we can find delight in the prosperity of our brothers and sisters. This means our joy is multiplied!

Stanza Six

**And if our fellowship below
in Jesus be so sweet,
what heights of rapture shall we know
when round his throne we meet!**

Scripture

Let us think of ways to motivate one another to acts of love and good works. And let us not neglect our meeting together, as some people do, but encourage one another, especially now that the day of his return is drawing near (Hebrews 10:24-25).

Meditation

Why should we be part of a church? Because it gets us ready for the return of Jesus. The fellowship we enjoy as Christians, having a new family to share our burdens, prepares us for the day when Jesus comes back, raises us from the dead, and begins a new heaven and earth.

We cannot fully imagine what that new existence will be like, but we do get a glimpse of it in the life we share together now in Christ. We regularly assemble as God's people to encourage one another in our trust in the Lord. That walking together in His path extends into eternity. Together we will gather around the throne of God and give Him the praise He deserves.

That's why we praise Him together now. We are practicing for that day.

For Reflection

1. How can we be united with Christians who disagree with us?
2. When was the last time you shared in another's joys?
3. How does being part of the church get us ready for the return of Jesus?

Live the Hymn

1. With the help of the Spirit, try to have as much joy in the good fortune of others as you have in your own blessings.
2. List the ways that church has blessed you.

Prayer

Fill us with the unspeakable joy that comes from sharing with others, O Lord.

Day Twenty-One:
Blow ye the Trumpet, Blow (I)

STANZA ONE

**Blow ye the trumpet, blow!
The gladly solemn sound
let all the nations know,
to earth's remotest bound:
The year of jubilee is come;
return, ye ransomed sinners, home;**

SCRIPTURE

Blow the trumpets in times of gladness, too, sounding them at your annual festivals and at the beginning of each month. And blow the trumpets over your burnt offerings and peace offerings. The trumpets will remind your God of his covenant with you. I am the Lord your God (Numbers 10:10).

MEDITATION

Trumpets in the Bible are not for playing tunes, but for getting attention. They are much like those annoying alerts on our televisions or phones. They tell us something significant is happening. Trumpets in the Bible announce the powerful acts of God—defeating enemies, making covenants, and calling His people to assemble. When you heard the trumpet, you knew God was about to act in a powerful way.

Stanza Two

Jesus, our great High Priest,
has full atonement made;
ye weary spirits, rest;
ye mournful souls, be glad:
The year of jubilee is come;
return, ye ransomed sinners, home;

Scripture

Therefore, it was necessary for him to be made in every respect like us, his brothers and sisters, so that he could be our merciful and faithful High Priest before God. Then he could offer a sacrifice that would take away the sins of the people (Hebrews 2:17).

Meditation

Every fifty years Israel was to celebrate the jubilee, a time when they returned land to its original owners, freed slaves, forgave debts, and rested. It was a restart, a new beginning for God's people.

Jesus has given us a permanent jubilee. Through His death and resurrection He gives us title to the new heaven and earth. He frees us from our slavery to sin. He forgives the debt we owed to God. He gives us a rest with Him.

All He asks is that we return to Him.

Stanza Three

**Extol the Lamb of God,
the sacrificial Lamb;
redemption thro' his blood
throughout the world proclaim:
The year of jubilee is come;
return, ye ransomed sinners, home;**

Scripture

The next day John saw Jesus coming toward him and said, "Look! The Lamb of God who takes away the sin of the world!" (John 1:29).

Meditation

When God's people thought of lambs, they thought of sacrifice. The first sacrifice offered to God in the Bible is a lamb, offered by Abel (Genesis 4:4). Abraham offers lambs (Genesis 22:8).

Lambs are sacrificed at the first Passover (Exodus 12:1-20). The giving of lambs was an important part of the sacrificial system of Israel.

So it is significant that the first words used by John the Baptist to describe Jesus are, "Lamb of God." John could have described Jesus as the conquering king. That was the kind of Messiah the people expected. Instead, he describes Him as a suffering Messiah who will redeem the world.

So we also extol the Sacrificial Lamb who saves us and the rest of the world. We spread that good news to all the earth.

For Reflection

1. What do trumpets signify in the Bible?
2. What happened in the year of Jubilee?
3. Why is it important that Jesus came as a lamb?

Live the Hymn

1. When you hear an alert on your phone today, think of the announcement of the work of God in Jesus.
2. Forgive someone a debt today as God's people forgave debts in the year of Jubilee.

Prayer

Jesus, in jubilation we return to you in freedom and rest.

Day Twenty-Two:
Blow ye the Trumpet, Blow (II)

Stanza Four

Ye slaves of sin and hell,
your liberty receive;
and safe in Jesus dwell,
and blest in Jesus live:
The year of jubilee is come;
return, ye ransomed sinners, home

Scripture

All of us used to live that way, following the passionate desires and inclinations of our sinful nature. By our very nature we were subject to God's anger, just like everyone else (Ephesians 2:3).

Meditation

Those of us raised as Christians cannot remember a time when we did not know Jesus and love Him. *Jesus Loves Me*, is the first song some of us learned.

So it is difficult to think that we were ever slaves of sin and hell, subject to God's anger. But think of what we would be without Jesus. Without Him we would be controlled by our ever-changing and insatiable desires. We would be victims of every craze and fashion that our culture bombards us with. And God would be angry at us because He loves us, just as parents are angry when their children do what is self-destructive, yet do not stop loving them.

But Jesus has freed us from that slavery to self and the world.

Stanza Five

**Ye who have sold for naught
your heritage above,
receive it back unbought,
the gift of Jesus' love:
The year of jubilee is come;
return, ye ransomed sinners, home**

Scripture

Make sure that no one is immoral or godless like Esau, who traded his birthright as the firstborn son for a single meal (Hebrews 12:16).

Meditation

I remember my frustration when I first heard the story of Esau in Sunday School (Genesis 25:29–34). How could anyone be so dumb as to trade their birthright for a bowl of soup?

This hymn compares us to Esau. We were created in the image of God. We were born to be God's beloved children. But, like Esau, we traded all that away for brief pleasures.

The good news is that Jesus returns all that to us, canceling the bad trade we had made. As in the year of jubilee, when God's people have their land returned to them, even if they had sold it, so Jesus restores all that we had lost to sin.

Stanza Six

**The gospel trumpet hear,
the news of heav'nly grace;
and, saved from earth, appear
before your Savior's face:
The year of jubilee is come;
return, ye ransomed sinners, home**

Scripture

And he will send out his angels with the mighty blast of a trumpet, and they will gather his chosen ones from all over the world—from the farthest ends of the earth and heaven (Matthew 24:31).

Meditation

God's people listened closely for the sound of the trumpet that would call them to assemble, to sacrifice, and to begin the year of jubilee. The trumpet brought good news!

We listen for another trumpet, a final call to the ultimate good news. That trumpet announces the return of Jesus. He will bring with Him those faithful who have died (1 Thessalonians 4:14). He will gather His people from all the corners of the earth. He will change their bodies to be like His glorious resurrected body (Philippians 3:21). He will bring the New Jerusalem from above, creating a new heaven and earth where we will be with Him forever.

Each day we listen for that trumpet call with great anticipation. We listen through every act that shows our love for God and for neighbor. Jubilee is come!

For Reflection

1. In what way were we slaves to the world before trusting in Jesus?

2. How, like Esau, did we sell our spiritual heritage cheaply?
3. What does it mean that Jesus will return with the sound of a trumpet?

Live the Hymn

1. Read about contemporary slavery. Then think of what it means to be free in Christ.
2. Alert others to the good news of Jesus.

Prayer

Savior, blow the trumpet! Return soon! Bring us home!

Day Twenty-Three:
You Servants of God

STANZA ONE

You servants of God, your Master proclaim,
and publish abroad his wonderful name;
the name all-victorious of Jesus extol;
his kingdom is glorious and rules over all.

SCRIPTURE

And whatever you do, in word or deed, do everything in the name of the Lord Jesus, giving thanks to God the Father through him (Colossians 3:17, ESV).

MEDITATION

There are names of world rulers through history that everyone knows—Alexander, Caesar, Charlemagne, Napoleon, Cleopatra, Victoria, and others. But there is one name above all others who rules all countries.

As servants of God, we proclaim that name, Jesus, not only as our Master, but also as the Master of the world.

STANZA TWO

God rules in the height, almighty to save;
though hid from our sight, his presence we have;
the great congregation his triumph shall sing,
ascribing salvation to Jesus our King

Scripture

No one has ever seen God. But the unique One, who is himself God, is near to the Father's heart. He has revealed God to us (John 1:18).

Meditation

God is greater than the infinite universe. He is beyond our sight. He is beyond our imagination.

So how can we know God? How can we know what God thinks of us? And how can we have a relationship with this fathomless God?

Not by trying. Human effort alone can never bring us to God, or God to us. We know the hidden God only because He has revealed Himself in creation, in Scripture, and most fully in Jesus. God became one of us so that we might know Him, know that He loves us, and that we might be like Him.

With countless others, we praise the Presence of God in Jesus.

Stanza Three

"Salvation to God, who sits on the throne!"
let all cry aloud, and honor the Son;
the praises of Jesus the angels proclaim,
fall down on their faces and worship the Lamb.

Scripture

After this I saw a vast crowd, too great to count, from every nation and tribe and people and language, standing in front of the throne and before the Lamb. They were clothed in white robes and held palm branches in their hands. And they were shouting with a great roar, "Salvation comes from our God who sits on the throne and from the Lamb!" (Revelation 7:9-10).

Meditation

The book of Revelation is a series of visions. Like great art, it is to be seen and appreciated, not studied to death or explained away.

So picture in your mind the greatest crowd you can imagine, a gathering that no one can count. Imagine the most diverse mass of people you can, from every nation and tribe, every shape and color, speaking every language and dialect. In your mind's eye see them united in one act—praising the Almighty God on His throne and the Lamb of God who takes away the sins of the world.

Now join them in praise!

Stanza Four

Then let us adore and give him his right:
all glory and power, all wisdom and might,
all honor and blessing with angels above
and thanks never ceasing for infinite love.

Scripture

And all the angels were standing around the throne and around the elders and the four living beings. And they fell before the throne with their faces to the ground and worshiped God. They sang, "Amen! Blessing and glory and wisdom and thanksgiving and honor and power and strength belong to our God forever and ever! Amen." (Revelation 7:11-12).

Meditation

The picture of worship around the Great Throne continues. Now the vast crowd increases by twenty-four elders—twelve tribes and twelve apostles—representing the people of God throughout the ages. Strange creatures are there, standing for all the created order. Then come the angels, being so awesome that humans are tempted to worship them. But they fall down and worship the One on the Throne and the Lamb.

Can you see it? Then let that astounding vision be with you in the ordinary moments of this day. That view of what is to come gives us strength to overcome all evil.

For Reflection

1. What other words other than "master" do we use to describe those who have authority over us?
2. Why is it important that the crowd that praises God is from every nation and tribe and people and language?
3. Why is it important that the angels, elders, and creatures join in that praise?

Live the Hymn

1. Since it is hard for us to relate to the word "master," try calling God your boss, director, or supervisor as you pray to Him.
2. Like those who worship in the Book of Revelation, fall face down before the Lord.

Prayer

Lord, open our eyes to see you on the throne, ruling the world in love.

Day Twenty-Four:
And Can it Be

STANZA ONE

And can it be that I should gain
An int'rest in the Savior's blood?
Died He for me, who caused His pain?
For me, who Him to death pursued?
Amazing love! how can it be
That Thou, my God, should die for me?

SCRIPTURE

But God showed his great love for us by sending Christ to die for us while we were still sinners (Romans 5:8).

MEDITATION

Who put Jesus on the cross? We can blame some of the Jewish religious leaders or Pilate and the Roman authorities. But our sins nailed Jesus to the cross.

For those of us who think of ourselves as good people, that is hard to admit. Yes, we fall short of what God intends for us, but we can't imagine crucifying our Savior. Like Pilate, we may (at least mentally) wash our hands clean from His blood.

God in the flesh suffered and died for our sins. If we can admit that and feel the full force of it, then we can sing of that amazing love.

STANZA TWO

'Tis mystery all! Th'Immortal dies!
Who can explore His strange design?
In vain the firstborn seraph tries
To sound the depths of love divine!
'Tis mercy all! let earth adore,
Let angel minds inquire no more.

SCRIPTURE

And now this Good News has been announced to you by those who preached in the power of the Holy Spirit sent from heaven. It is all so wonderful that even the angels are eagerly watching these things happen. (1 Peter 1:12).

MEDITATION

Years ago I heard a radio broadcast of an imaginary scene in heaven. Those who had been redeemed by Jesus gathered around the throne of God to praise Him for their salvation. What struck me most was when the narrator said, "The angels who had never sinned look on in bewilderment because they do not know what it means to be redeemed."

The good news that the Immortal God became human and died for us is so amazingly strange that the angels cannot fathom it. The mystery of God's love for humanity is beyond their comprehension.

STANZA THREE

He left His Father's throne above,
So free, so infinite His grace;
Emptied Himself of all but love,
And bled for Adam's helpless race;

> 'Tis mercy all, immense and free;
> For, O my God, it found out me

SCRIPTURE

Have this mind among yourselves, which is yours in Christ Jesus, who, though he was in the form of God, did not count equality with God a thing to be grasped, but emptied himself, by taking the form of a servant, being born in the likeness of men (Philippians 2:5-7, ESV).

MEDITATION

How can Jesus of Nazareth be God? God is infinite. Humans are finite. God knows everything. Jesus had to learn (Luke 2:52, Hebrews 5:8). God is everywhere. Jesus could only be one place at a time. God is immortal. Jesus died on the cross.

How can Jesus be human and still be God? There is a mystery here, but the answer lies in the willingness of Jesus to empty Himself. To be human like one of us, He gave up His infinite knowledge, His rule over all creation, and even His immortality. He could have refused. He could have demanded His rights as the Almighty God. But He emptied Himself for us.

STANZA FOUR

> **Long my imprisoned spirit lay**
> **Fast bound in sin and nature's night;**
> **Thine eye diffused a quick'ning ray,**
> **I woke, the dungeon flamed with light;**
> **My chains fell off, my heart was free;**
> **I rose, went forth and followed Thee.**

Scripture

Jesus answered them, "Truly, truly, I say to you, everyone who practices sin is a slave to sin. The slave does not remain in the house forever; the son remains forever. So if the Son sets you free, you will be free indeed" (John 8:34-36 ESV).

Meditation

I cannot imagine what it would be like to be a slave. However, I have felt trapped in situations where I could not escape. I once thought we would lose our house because of a clause in our mortgage. I've been in soul-crushing jobs that I thought I could not leave. Perhaps you've felt the same.

Is sin that kind of slavery? It is if we think of sin like we think of addiction. We are powerless to overcome it on our own. The great news is that Jesus freed us from our prison cell, our slavery to sin, so we might be free indeed.

Stanza Five

No condemnation now I dread;
Jesus, and all in Him is mine!
Alive in Him, my living Head,
And clothed in righteousness divine,
Bold I approach th'eternal throne,
And claim the crown, through Christ my own.

Scripture

So let us come boldly to the throne of our gracious God. There we will receive his mercy, and we will find grace to help us when we need it most (Hebrews 4:16).

Meditation

Knowing our failures, weaknesses, and sins, how can we stand before a Holy God? To even imagine that we can do so seems like pride and presumption.

Yet we are called to come boldly into the very throne room of the Holy One.

We can do so because we do not come alone. We come with the one who gave Himself in our place. In a sense, we do not approach the Holy, Jesus does. He clothes us with His righteousness. When the Almighty looks down at us from His throne, He sees Jesus, His beloved Son. He sees us as His beloved daughters and sons.

So we come to Him, not with shame, but with confidence that we will receive mercy and grace.

For Reflection

1. How can we understand redemption better than angels can understand it?
2. Have you ever been enslaved or addicted to something? How has Jesus set you free from that?
3. Why are we confident in approaching God?

Live the Hymn

1. Meditate on God dying for you.
2. As you put on your clothes, think of being clothed with Christ.

Prayer

Holy God, may we come before you this day certain of your love.

Day Twenty-Five:
O Love Divine, What Hast Thou Done?

Stanza One

O Love divine, what hast thou done!
The immortal God hath died for me!
The Father's co-eternal Son
bore all my sins upon the tree;
the immortal God for me hath died!
My Lord, my Love is crucified:

Scripture

For in Christ lives all the fullness of God in a human body (Colossians 2:9).

Meditation

One can imagine different ways that God could have saved humanity. He could have simply pronounced us saved. But would that have fully expressed the love of God? He could have continued the system of animal sacrifices for sin, but would those sacrifices have been adequate to make up for human rebellion? He could have sent prophets or angels to suffer in our place.

Instead, God Himself became flesh. The co-eternal Son, who created the world and rules all things, became human like us. What's more, He was crucified for our sins. That shows both the depth of our rejection of God and the extreme of His love for us.

So we praise Him for his unfathomable delight in us!

Stanza Two

**Is crucified for me and you,
to bring us rebels back to God;
believe, believe the record true,
we all are bought with Jesu' blood,
pardon for all flows from his side:
my Lord, my Love, is crucified.**

Scripture

For even the Son of Man came not to be served but to serve others and to give his life as a ransom for many (Mark 10:45).

Meditation

Presidents often issue pardons. We wonder why they pardon some and not others. Are the pardons the result of political favors or are they acts of justice and mercy?

It is particularly hard to pardon those who rebel against the government. Even if pardoned, some still consider them enemies. And there is always the worry that they will rebel again.

Sin is not just making mistakes. It is rebellion against God. Through the cross God gave free pardons to us rebels. We respond with loyalty to Him, and we in turn accept others who are pardoned. We are no longer enemies of God or enemies of others.

Stanza Three

**Then let us sit beneath the cross,
and gladly catch the healing stream,
all things for him account but loss,**

> **and give up all our hearts to him;**
> **of nothing think or speak beside:**
> **my Lord, my Love is crucified.**

SCRIPTURE

Yes, everything else is worthless when compared with the infinite value of knowing Christ Jesus my Lord. For his sake I have discarded everything else, counting it all as garbage, so that I could gain Christ (Philippians 3:8).

MEDITATION

What do you want on your tombstone? How will your obituary read?

Many want others to remember their accomplishments. They would place their titles, awards, and achievements in their obituaries. Others desire their family to remember them, so they place their names there.

Here is the ultimate line for your tombstone or obituary: "(insert your name here) knew Christ Jesus as Lord." All the other successes of life-—whether family or job or even fame and fortune—are garbage next to this.

FOR REFLECTION

1. Why did God send his Son to redeem us instead of saving us another way?
2. Why did we need to be pardoned?
3. What should be our greatest accomplishment in life?

LIVE THE HYMN

1. Imagine being in prison and then being pardoned. How would you feel? Try to feel the same today about being pardoned by Jesus.
2. Take some time to meditate on the crucifixion.

PRAYER

Crucified Lord, we bow in awe of your grace.

Day Twenty-Six:
'Tis Finished!

STANZA ONE

**'Tis finished! The Messiah dies-
cut off for sins, but not His own;
accomplished is the sacrifice-
the great redeeming work is done.**

SCRIPTURE

But he was pierced for our rebellion, crushed for our sins. He was beaten so we could be whole. He was whipped so we could be healed (Isaiah 53:5).

MEDITATION

The description of the Suffering Servant in Isaiah 53 is so similar to the experience of Jesus on the cross that we can't understand how almost everyone in Jesus's time missed it. The idea of a suffering Messiah was so foreign to their reading of the Bible. The Messiah was to be a conquering king who would rule with justice. A suffering and dead Messiah made no sense.

That's why the disciples could not understand when Jesus repeatedly told them that He would be rejected and killed. Only after the resurrection did they see this passage in Isaiah as a description of Jesus.

We may think the disciples slow to understand, but are we any better? Do we understand that we are to take up our crosses and suffer with Jesus?

Stanza Two

**The veil is rent; in Christ alone
the living way to heav'n is seen;
the middle wall is broken down,
and all mankind may enter in.**

Scripture

Then Jesus shouted out again, and he released his spirit. At that moment, the curtain in the sanctuary of the Temple was torn in two, from top to bottom (Matthew 27:50-51).

Meditation

The tearing of the curtain in the temple may seem like a small detail of the crucifixion story, however, its symbolism is profound. This was the heavy curtain or veil that separated the Holy Place from the Most Holy Place. That inner room was so holy because the Ark of the Covenant, topped by the throne of God, the mercy seat, was there. It was so holy that only the high priest could enter it once a year on the day of atonement.

At the death of Jesus, the curtain tears from top to bottom. It is God who rips away the barrier between Himself and us. We can now approach His throne of mercy because the death of Jesus gives us a clear path.

Stanza Three

**'Tis finished! All my guilt and pain,
I want no sacrifice beside;
for me, for me the Lamb is slain,
'tis finished! I am justified.**

SCRIPTURE

A jar of sour wine was sitting there, so they soaked a sponge in it, put it on a hyssop branch, and held it up to his lips. When Jesus had tasted it, he said, "It is finished!" Then he bowed his head and gave up his spirit (John 19:29-30).

MEDITATION

When Jesus said, "It is finished," He meant more than the cartoonish, "That's all, folks!" He meant that His work of redemption was completed. That work began before the world began (Ephesians 1:4). That work continued through the entire story of the Old Testament—creation, sin, Abraham, Moses, Israel, exile, and return. Jesus, the Word made flesh, embodied that redemptive work throughout His ministry of healing and teaching.

But it was on the cross that the liberating act of God through Jesus reached its climax. The Lamb, the ultimate sacrifice, gives His life for the sins of the world. No other sacrifice is needed. He conquers sin and death. It is finished!

STANZA FOUR

**The reign of sin and death is o'er;
all grace is now to sinners giv'n;
and, lo! I plead th'atoning blood,
and in Thy right I claim my heav'n.**

SCRIPTURE

Unlike those other high priests, he does not need to offer sacrifices every day. They did this for their own sins first and then for the sins of the people. But Jesus did this once for all when he offered himself as the sacrifice for the people's sins (Hebrews 7:27).

MEDITATION

We are a people who insist on our rights. We vigorously demand those rights when we vote and through our legal system. "Don't tread on me."

So we boldly claim our right to heaven.

Really? It seems awfully presumptuous to say such a thing. Salvation is about grace, not rights. But if we ask a different question, it all begins to make sense. Does Jesus have a right to heaven? Of course He does! He is the Son of God. If He has that right, then as His body, we do too.

FOR REFLECTION

1. Why was it so hard for those in his day to accept Jesus as a suffering Messiah?
2. What did Jesus mean when He said, "It is finished"?
3. Do we have a right to heaven? If so, how?

LIVE THE HYMN

1. Find a way to suffer with Jesus today.
2. Pray, knowing that Jesus has removed all barriers between you and God.

PRAYER

Jesus, you are in us and we are in you. May we enjoy our heaven together!

Day Twenty-Seven:
Arise my Soul, Arise (I)

Stanza One

Arise, my soul, arise,
Shake off thy guilty fears;
The bleeding sacrifice
In my behalf appears;
Before the throne my surety stands;
My name is written on his hands.

Scripture

So now there is no condemnation for those who belong to Christ Jesus (Romans 8:1).

Meditation

From the title of this book, you might guess that this is my favorite Charles Wesley hymn. Many of the phrases of the hymn speak to me, especially, "cast off thy guilty fears." I was raised in a church that reminded us often of our guilt. I had enough shame for the sins I did commit, but the preaching I heard even made me feel guilty about things that were not really sins!

Thank God we had hymns like this and not just preaching! The hymns of grace we sang spoke more deeply to my guilty heart than did the sermons I heard. They empowered me to shake off my fear that I was not good enough for God. They taught me that no one is good enough, but that the bleeding sacrifice of Jesus assures our soul that we belong to God.

Stanza Two

**He ever lives above
For me to intercede;
His all-redeeming love
His precious blood to plead;
His blood atoned for all our race
And sprinkles now the throne of grace.**

Scripture

Just think how much more the blood of Christ will purify our consciences from sinful deeds so that we can worship the living God. For by the power of the eternal Spirit, Christ offered himself to God as a perfect sacrifice for our sins (Hebrews 9:14).

Meditation

A clean conscience.

What a gift that is! Many of us are cursed with being overly conscientious. We constantly doubt our motives and question our decisions.

The precious blood of Jesus completely purifies our consciences. We no longer have to rethink our every action. A clean conscience sets us free to think less often of ourselves in order to serve others around us. We remain free from guilt and shame because the one who shed His blood for us is also the one who ever lives to intercede for us.

Stanza Three

**Five bleeding wounds he bears,
Received on Calvary;
They pour effectual prayers,**

They strongly speak for me;
Forgive him, oh forgive, they cry,
Nor let that ransomed sinner die.

Scripture

Then he said to Thomas, "Put your finger here, and look at my hands. Put your hand into the wound in my side. Don't be faithless any longer. Believe!" "My Lord and my God!" Thomas exclaimed (John 20:27-28)

Meditation

The resurrected Jesus showed Thomas his five wounds—right hand, left hand, right foot, left foot, and his side.

What's the significance of these wounds? They show that the Jesus God raised from the dead was the same one who was crucified. Even more, as by faith we see those wounds, we meditate on the suffering of Jesus for us. He suffered to heal the wounds of the entire world. Those wounds show that the resurrected Jesus is still human as we are, now with a glorified spiritual body like the one we will have some day.

For Reflection

1. How are guilt and fear related?
2. How does it feel to have a clean conscience?
3. Why are the wounds of Jesus significant?

Live the Hymn

1. Take the time to think about the wounds of Jesus.
2. Try to take the weight of guilt off someone else's shoulders.

Prayer

God of love, give us the surety to shake off our guilty fears.

Day Twenty-Eight:
Arise My Soul, Arise (II)

Stanza Four

The Father hears him pray,
His dear Anointed One;
He cannot turn away
The presence of his Son;
His Spirit answers to the blood
And tells me I am born of God.

Scripture

So we have these three witnesses—the Spirit, the water, and the blood—and all three agree. And this is what God has testified: He has given us eternal life, and this life is in his Son (1 John 5:7-8, 11).

Meditation

Spirit, water, and blood. Jesus said we must be born of water and Spirit (John 3:5). In the water of baptism, we receive the Holy Spirit (Acts 2:38, 1 Corinthians 12:13). In baptism, we come in contact with the blood of Christ. The Spirit makes us holy through the cleansing blood of Jesus (1 Peter 1:2).

These three witnesses confirm the sure testimony of God that we have eternal life. If we ever find ourselves doubting our salvation, let us remember that we are baptized, that we have the Holy Spirit, and we are made clean by the blood of Jesus.

Stanza Five

**My God is reconciled,
His pard'ning voice I hear;
He owns me for his child;
I can no longer fear;
With confidence I now draw nigh,
And Father, Abba Father, cry!**

Scripture

And because we are his children, God has sent the Spirit of his Son into our hearts, prompting us to call out, "Abba, Father" (Galatians 4:6).

Meditation

When Jesus was baptized, He heard a voice from heaven say, "This is the Son whom I love."

When we were baptized we heard the same voice. By faith we heard God call our name and say we were His beloved son or daughter.

Every day, we must continue to listen to that voice. There are so many other voices around us and inside us, telling us we are not worthy of God's love. Do not listen to them! Hear only the voice that pardons us, removes all our fears, and asks us to come near to Him. Listen to voice of our Abba, our Father.

For Reflection

1. How are Spirit, water, and blood connected?
2. What does it mean that these three are witnesses?
3. When do you hear the voice of God?

Live the Hymn

1. Take the time to be alone with God and listen to His voice.
2. When you pray, call God "Abba."

PRAYER

Abba, Father, open our hearts to your loving voice.

Day Twenty-Nine:
Forever Here My Rest Shall Be

STANZA ONE

Forever here my rest shall be,
Close to Thy bleeding side.
This all my hope, and all my plea.
"For me the Saviour died."

SCRIPTURE

He is so rich in kindness and grace that he purchased our freedom with the blood of his Son and forgave our sins (Ephesians 1:7).

MEDITATION

Unless you are a hunter, work with livestock, or are in the medical profession, you likely do not see much blood. I confess that I do not like the sight of blood, especially my own.

So why is there so much blood in the Bible? Bloody sacrifices, bloody battles, and the constant theme of the blood of Jesus—these are on almost every page.

We know the answer. Blood is life. We city dwellers might ignore "Nature red in tooth and claw," as the poet Alfred, Lord Tennyson (1809-1892) puts it. But most people live with blood in some form each day.

Yes, blood can mean death, but if you need a transfusion, blood is life. And what we need and what we get from Jesus is the blood that gives life.

Stanza Two

My dying Saviour, and my God,
Fountain for guilt and sin,
Sprinkle me ever with Thy blood,
And cleanse, and keep me clean.

Scripture

God the Father knew you and chose you long ago, and his Spirit has made you holy. As a result, you have obeyed him and have been cleansed by the blood of Jesus Christ (1 Peter 1:2).

Meditation

When I bleed I try to stop it immediately. Then I quickly wash the blood away, but the Bible says blood makes us clean. How does that work?

In the Old Testament, the blood of animals purified the people of God. The idea may be that the life-blood of the animal took the place of the blood of sinful humans. We owed God a death for separating ourselves from Him, the source of all life. Instead of demanding our death, the Lord allowed an animal to substitute. This showed the seriousness of sin. It cost a life.

In a much fuller way, the lifeblood of Jesus, given instead of our blood, makes us clean from sin and brings us new life. Our sins were not small things we got wrong; they were symptoms of turning our hearts away from God. Blood shows the weight of sin and salvation.

Stanza Three

Wash me, and make me thus Thine own;
Wash me, and mine Thou art;

> **Wash me, but not my feet alone—-**
> **My hands, my head, my heart.**

SCRIPTURE

All glory to him who loves us and has freed us from our sins by shedding his blood for us (Revelation 1:5).

MEDITATION

This verse of the hymn reflects the story of Peter refusing to have Jesus wash his feet. When Jesus tells him, "Unless I wash you, you won't belong to me," Peter then asks him to wash his hands, head, and feet (John 13:8-9). You have to admire Peter's desire to belong completely to Jesus.

The hymn adds heart to the list of what needs to be washed. The blood of Jesus makes us completely clean. What's more, Jesus washed the disciples' feet not only to make them clean and so they would belong to Him, He did it as an example to them, that they should wash the feet of others.

If we serve others as Jesus served, we bring that cleansing blood to them.

STANZA FOUR

> **The atonement of Thy blood apply,**
> **Till faith to sight improve;**
> **Till hope in full fruition die,**
> **And all my soul be love.**

SCRIPTURE

Under the old system, the blood of goats and bulls and the ashes of a heifer could cleanse people's bodies from ceremonial impurity. Just think how much more the blood of Christ will purify our consciences from sinful deeds so that we can worship the living God. For by the power of the eternal Spirit, Christ offered himself to God as a perfect sacrifice for our sins (Hebrews 9:13-14).

MEDITATION

How do we know that our sins are perfectly forgiven? How can we be sure that our consciences are clean?

Only by trusting in the blood of Christ, given for us through the power of the Spirit.

But the day will come when we do not have to rely on trust. The day is dawning when faith will be sight. The day will come when we no longer have hope because hope has become reality. The day will come when all that remains is love (1 Corinthians 13:13).

FOR REFLECTION

1. Why is there so much talk of blood in the Bible?
2. We usually think of blood as staining, not cleaning. How does the blood of Jesus make us clean?
3. Why will faith and hope disappear when Jesus comes?

LIVE THE HYMN

1. Since Jesus has washed us clean, wash someone else's feet today by serving them.
2. Rest today in the assurance of your cleansing through the blood of Jesus.

PRAYER

Bleeding Jesus, make us trust that we are completely clean by your sacrifice.

Day Thirty:
Christ the Lord is Risen Today (I)

STANZA ONE

Christ the Lord is risen today, Alleluia!
Earth and heaven in chorus say, Alleluia!
Raise your joys and triumphs high, Alleluia!
Sing, ye heavens, and earth reply, Alleluia!

SCRIPTURE

Then the angel spoke to the women. "Don't be afraid!" he said. "I know you are looking for Jesus, who was crucified. He isn't here! He is risen from the dead, just as he said would happen. Come, see where his body was lying" (Matthew 28:5-6).

MEDITATION

The women at the tomb expected to find a dead body. Their hopes in Jesus as the Messiah had been crushed by his crucifixion and death, but they find no body at all; at least not a dead body. Instead, they find angels. As angels announced the birth of Jesus, so now they announce his resurrection. But the ongoing telling of this great news begins with these women and continues with all the disciples of Jesus.

So we say with unbounded joy, "Christ is risen." With earth and heaven we sing "Alleluia." We sing and shout the news, not just with words but with every breath and every act of our lives. Christ is risen. He is risen indeed!

STANZA TWO

Love's redeeming work is done, Alleluia!
Fought the fight, the battle won, Alleluia!
Death in vain forbids him rise, Alleluia!
Christ has opened paradise, Alleluia!

SCRIPTURE

And since we died with Christ, we know we will also live with him. We are sure of this because Christ was raised from the dead, and he will never die again. Death no longer has any power over him (Romans 6:8-9).

MEDITATION

The resurrection shows that Jesus has conquered death not just for Himself but for everyone. He defeats death not by force but by being willing to die for others. He fights with the most powerful weapon of all—sacrificial love.

As death has no power over Jesus, so it has no power over us. It may not seem that way. We still have a strong, sometimes overwhelming fear of death, but through Jesus, we know that death is not the end. Paradise with our loving God is what we have through death and resurrection. The path through death was frightening even for Jesus. That's why He prayed that the cup of suffering might pass. But through His faithfulness to God's will, we also can trust.

STANZA THREE

Lives again our glorious King, Alleluia!
Where, O death, is now thy sting? Alleluia!
Once he died our souls to save, Alleluia!
Where's thy victory, boasting grave? Alleluia!

Scripture

Then, when our dying bodies have been transformed into bodies that will never die, this Scripture will be fulfilled: "Death is swallowed up in victory. O death, where is your victory? O death, where is your sting?" (1 Corinthians 15:54-55).

Meditation

Looking forward to Paradise with the Lord may sound like "Pie in the sky when you die by and by." It can be a shallow retreat from the reality of suffering and death.

The hope of resurrection is much more powerful than a fond wish for something after death. It is a sure conviction that the one who raised Jesus from the dead will also raise our bodies. We do not deny the reality of death but reject its finality. Death itself will be destroyed (1 Corinthians 15:26).

So the sting of death, the fear that we will no longer exist and that this life was just a dream, is swallowed up in assurance of a new life beyond our imaginations.

For Reflection

1. How do we join with angels in proclaiming the good news?
2. How does the resurrection of Jesus help us overcome our fear of death?
3. What comes to mind when you think of "paradise?"

Live the Hymn

1. As you pray alone today, shout "Alleluia" out loud to show your joy at the resurrection.
2. Share the news of the resurrection of Jesus with someone.

Prayer

Risen Lord, fill us with the good news of resurrection and life.

Day Thirty-One:
Christ the Lord is Risen Today (II)

Stanza Four

Soar we now where Christ has led, Alleluia!
Following our exalted Head, Alleluia!
Made like him, like him we rise, Alleluia!
Ours the cross, the grave, the skies, Alleluia!

Scripture

God has put all things under the authority of Christ and has made him head over all things for the benefit of the church (Ephesians 1:22).

Meditation

A body does much better when connected to and ruled by the head. When we confess that Jesus is head of the church, we mean He is both the authority that rules us and the source of our life. It is another way of saying, "Jesus is Lord."

Our connection to our Lord is as personal and intimate as the connection between our own head and body. Although personal, our relationship with Jesus is also communal. The church, not just individuals, is His body.

That means we share in the identity of Jesus. We are (or will be) what He is. We go with Him through the cross, the tomb, and resurrection. The absolute power that He has is for our benefit. His resurrection and glorification are for us.

Stanza Five

Hail the Lord of earth and heaven, Alleluia!
Praise to thee by both be given, Alleluia!
Thee we greet triumphant now, Alleluia!
Hail the Resurrection, thou, Alleluia!

Scripture

But thank God! He has made us his captives and continues to lead us along in Christ's triumphal procession. Now he uses us to spread the knowledge of Christ everywhere, like a sweet perfume (2 Corinthians 2:14).

Meditation

It is strange to celebrate captivity. It all depends on who captures you. We serve the resurrected Jesus who triumphed over all the evil powers, including death. By that victory, He captured us from sin and death. Our capture is thus a rescue.

But we are still captives. We do not belong to ourselves but to Jesus alone. And the one who enslaves us now is the one who gives us true freedom. He has not only been raised from the dead, but he is the Resurrection itself (John 11:25).

As slaves of Jesus, we spread the good news of resurrection to those around us. We diffuse the sweet smell of the Savior wherever we go.

Stanza Six

King of glory, soul of bliss, Alleluia!
Everlasting life is this, Alleluia!
Thee to know, thy power to prove, Alleluia!
Thus to sing, and thus to love, Alleluia!

SCRIPTURE

And this is the way to have eternal life—to know you, the only true God, and Jesus Christ, the one you sent to earth (John 17:3).

MEDITATION

God is beyond us. He surpasses all knowledge. We cannot imagine what God is like.

So how can we know God? Only because He shows Himself to us. He shows Himself in creation. He shows Himself in the covenant He makes with us. He shows Himself in Scripture.

He does more than that. He becomes one of us. We know the only true God in the face of Jesus of Nazareth. And we see Jesus most fully in His resurrection and glorification. What's more, Jesus shows Himself to us in his Holy Spirit who lives in us.

We cannot completely know God, but we can genuinely know God. That intimate knowledge generates eternal life in us now, a life of songs and love. Each day we prove the power of the King of glory, living in us.

FOR REFLECTION

1. What does it mean that Jesus is our head?
2. How are we captives of Jesus? How has He released us from captivity?
3. How do we know God?

LIVE THE HYMN

1. Today imagine that Jesus is the head of your body, directing everything you do.
2. Write your own song about the resurrection.

PRAYER

God of bliss, we thank you for the life of song that springs from knowing you.

Day Thirty-Two:
Jesus Christ is Risen

STANZA ONE

**Jesus Christ is ris'n today, alleluia!
our triumphant holy day, alleluia!
who did once, upon the cross, alleluia!
suffer to redeem our loss, alleluia!**

SCRIPTURE

After Jesus rose from the dead early on Sunday morning, the first person who saw him was Mary Magdalene, the woman from whom he had cast out seven demons (Mark 16:9).

MEDITATION

We call Sunday, "the Lord's Day."

But isn't every day the Lord's day? Is there any day when we are outside of His presence and love?

Yes, the Lord Jesus is with us each moment of every day. But Sunday is the day of resurrection. It is the day when we celebrate with praise the empty tomb, the appearances to witnesses, and the triumph over death. It is the day we reenact the death, burial, and resurrection of Jesus in the Lord's Supper. It is the day we meet with fellow believers to praise and eat and encourage. It is more than a holiday. It is a holy day. A day each week that reminds us that every day belongs to our Redeemer.

Stanza Two

Hymns of praise then let us sing, alleluia!
unto Christ, our heav'nly King, alleluia!
who endured the cross and grave, alleluia!
sinners to redeem and save, alleluia!

Scripture

We do this by keeping our eyes on Jesus, the champion who initiates and perfects our faith. Because of the joy awaiting him, he endured the cross, disregarding its shame. Now he is seated in the place of honor beside God's throne (Hebrews 12:2).

Meditation

Some of the older folks at our church were complaining about their aches and pains. The oldest woman among them, who had been silent until this point, finally spoke up and said in a loud voice, "Just live with it!"

Some things simply have to be endured. Jesus endured the cross. He "put up with it." He took on both the pain and the shame of crucifixion, a criminal's death. He experienced the fullness of that suffering to redeem and save us.

He endured because by faith He could see the joy of resurrection awaiting Him. That's how we endure.

Stanza Three

But the pains which He endured, alleluia!
our salvation have procured; alleluia!
now above the sky He's King, alleluia!
where the angels ever sing: alleluia!

SCRIPTURE

Therefore, God elevated him to the place of highest honor and gave him the name above all other names (Philippians 2:9).

MEDITATION

The young woman at the haircutters greeted me with, "How would you like your hair today, sir." Her co-worker made fun of her for calling me sir. I guess she thought it was too old-fashioned. But I told my haircutter what I wanted and added "Thank you, ma'am."

We rarely use terms of respect in our culture. There's something good about that. It means we want to treat everyone equally.

But if we are not careful, that informality and sense of equality spills over into our relationship with Jesus. Yes, He is human as we are. Yes, He is our brother and friend. But He also is our King and Lord. His Name is above every name. We praise Him with the "Alleluia" because He rules our lives completely.

FOR REFFLECTION

1. Why is Sunday the Lord's day?
2. Why did Jesus have to endure the cross?
3. How does enduring the cross elevate the name of Jesus above all names?

LIVE THE HYMN

1. Be creative in making Sunday a day that is special to the Lord.
2. Let the endurance of Jesus allow you to endure the challenges you face.

PRAYER

Jesus, thank you for the gift of Sunday and every day.

Day Thirty-Three:
Come, Let us Join With One Accord

STANZA ONE

Come, let us join with one accord
In hymns around the throne!
This is the day our rising Lord
Hath made and called His own.

SCRIPTURE

It was the Lord's Day, and I was worshiping in the Spirit. Suddenly, I heard behind me a loud voice like a trumpet blast (Revelation 1:10).

MEDITATION

Every day we praise God for what He has done through Jesus. We worship God—Father, Son, and Spirit—with every breath and every action.

Generally, we do not assemble with other Christians every day. There is a special day, Sunday, when we meet with others who follow Jesus, our brothers and sisters in Christ. When we gather with them, the Lord Jesus is with us as we praise the One who sits on the eternal throne. In that assembly we draw closer to God and to one another through prayer, Bible study, hymns of praise, and the Supper of the Lord.

All of life is worship but not all of life is the family reunion we experience in the Spirit on the Lord's day. Nothing can take its place.

Stanza Two

This is the day that God hath blessed,
The brightest of the seven,
Type of that everlasting rest
The saints enjoy in heaven.

Scripture

So then, there remains a Sabbath rest for the people of God (Hebrews 4:9, ESV).

Meditation

Some people rest on Sunday. Some rest on another day. Many do not rest at all.

We need a sabbath, a day of rest. We need it because we are overworked and burnt out. We need it as a reminder that we are saved by grace, not by all we do. Remember that Jesus Himself often made time to rest and be alone with His Father (Matthew 14:22-23; Mark 1:35; Luke 5:16).

So the day of resurrection is also a day of rest, a day when we experience the new life that comes through Jesus. It is a day we share in the rest God has enjoyed since creation (Genesis 2:2). On that day we rest, worship, eat, and play in trust that God can run the world without us. That day we connect with the Lord and with others.

By embracing the gift of sabbath, we receive the resurrection life every day.

STANZA THREE

Then let us in His name sing on,
And hasten to that day
When our Redeemer shall come down,
And shadows pass away.

SCRIPTURE

And let us not neglect our meeting together, as some people do, but encourage one another, especially now that the day of his return is drawing near (Hebrews 10:25).

MEDITATION

The Christians described in the New Testament expected Jesus to come soon. They even prayed, "Lord, come quickly!" (1 Corinthians 16:22). Perhaps it was easier for them to have that expectation because it was only a few years since Jesus had ascended. Or perhaps it was easier because they were often suffering persecution and longed for Jesus to return and rule.

Two thousand years later, I don't find Christians as eager for His return. It's been a long time since He walked the earth. We have it so good now that we are not desperate for His coming. That's why, more than ever, we need to meet with other Christians who can encourage us to trust in the Lord's return. "Creation still groans in anticipation of the new heaven and earth he will bring" (Romans 8:22). We need to ache with the same anticipation.

Stanza Four

**Not one, but all our days below,
Let us in hymns employ;
And in our Lord rejoicing go
To His eternal joy.**

Scripture

Then he said to the crowd, "If any of you wants to be my follower, you must give up your own way, take up your cross daily, and follow me" (Luke 9:23).

Meditation

The great challenge of being a Christian is that it is so daily.

We get tired of doing the same old things every day. Cleaning, cooking, shaving, and all the other daily tasks at home. Not to mention the repetitive work we do at our jobs.

If we are honest, we admit it's the same way with our lives as Christians. We find ourselves praying the same prayers, singing the same hymns, reading the same Bible verses, and sinning the same sins.

If we live in light of the resurrection, we know that all things are new. Even the same old actions gain novelty in the light of the Risen Lord. He gives us the power not only to do great things for Him, but even to do the little things. We carry the cross daily with joy.

For Reflection

1. If all days belong to the Lord, then how can Sunday be the "Lord's Day"?
2. What can we do to make Sunday a day of rest?
3. Do you think often of the Second Coming of Jesus? Why or why not?

Live the Hymn

1. Make plans this Sunday to make the day a worshipful and restful day.
2. Start each day with the reminder that it belongs to the Lord.

Prayer

Lord Jesus, may we worship you at all times and assemble on your special day.

Day Thirty-Four:
I Know That my Redeemer Lives (I)

STANZA ONE

I know that my Redeemer lives,
And ever prays for me;
A token of His love He gives,
A pledge of liberty.

SCRIPTURE

And he has identified us as his own by placing the Holy Spirit in our hearts as the first installment that guarantees everything he has promised us (2 Corinthians 1:22).

MEDITATION

The hymn says Jesus has given us a token of His love, a pledge of liberty. Scripture says that Jesus has given the Holy Spirit as a first installment of His promises. A few translations say He has given the Spirit as a "pledge" of the promises.

"Token" and "pledge" were words associated with romance in Wesley's day. One might give the beloved an object, a token, to show love. We still do this when we give Valentine's Day presents. That token could also be a pledge of a deeper commitment that was to come, like an engagement ring.

In the same way, Jesus has given the Spirit to His bride, the church. The Spirit is a token of His love and a guarantee of His commitment to us as Redeemer.

Stanza Two

I find Him lifting up my head;
He brings salvation near;
His presence makes me free indeed,
And He will soon appear.

Scripture

But you, O Lord, are a shield around me; you are my glory, the one who holds my head high (Psalm 3:3).

Meditation

"Hold your head up!"

That's what we tell people when they have tried their best and failed. "You've done your best. You have nothing to be ashamed of. Hold your head up."

It's easier said than done. What happens when you have not done your best? How can you not bow your head in shame and discouragement?

The traditional setting of Psalm Three is when David is running from his own son, Absalom, who has rebelled against him and stolen his kingdom. Almost all of David's friends have deserted him. David hangs his head in despair.

Yet he knows there is One who will lift up his head.

Jesus is our Redeemer who lives, always prays for us, and lifts up our heads when we think everyone is against us.

Hold your head high!

For Reflection

1. Why would this hymn use the romantic language of love tokens to speak of our relationship with Jesus?

2. How does Jesus pledge or guarantee our liberty?
3. What does it mean that Jesus lifts up our heads?

Live the Hymn

1. Pray boldly today, knowing that Jesus prays for you.
2. This day hold up your head in confidence in the presence of Jesus in your life.

Prayer

Lord, we praise you as our Redeemer who gives us assurance of your love.

Day Thirty-Five:
I Know That my Redeemer Lives (II)

STANZA THREE

He wills that I should holy be,
What can withstand His will?
The counsel of His grace in me
He surely shall fulfill.

SCRIPTURE

But now you must be holy in everything you do, just as God who chose you is holy. For the Scriptures say, "You must be holy because I am holy" (1 Peter 1:15-16).

MEDITATION

We've all known people who were too holy. They let everyone else know how righteous they were. They condemned every sin (and sinner) in sight, yet were blind to their own faults.

Yet one cannot be too holy. Yes, one can be smug and judgmental. But holiness describes the character of God. To be genuinely holy means we reflect the compassion and love of God. We show mercy as He does. We forgive as we have been forgiven.

Our Redeemer Jesus shows us what the holiness of God looks like. He wills that we should be like Him.

We cannot stand against that will.

Stanza Four

Jesus, I hang upon Thy word;
I steadfastly believe
Thou wilt return and claim me, Lord,
And to Thyself receive.

Scripture

After that, he taught daily in the Temple, but the leading priests, the teachers of religious law, and the other leaders of the people began planning how to kill him. But they could think of nothing, because all the people hung on every word he said (Luke 19:47-48).

Meditation

What would it have been like to hear Jesus teach? Would we, like these people, hang on His every word? Would we have understood what He said? Would we have welcomed His teachings?

How about now? In the Four Gospels we have a great deal of the teaching of Jesus. Do we listen to those words with joy? Do we believe Him when He says that He has gone to prepare a place for us and will return to claim us, so we can be with Him forever (John 14:1-3)?

Stanza Five

When God is mine and I am His,
Of paradise possessed,
I taste unutterable bliss
And everlasting rest.

Scripture

Taste and see that the Lord is good. Oh, the joys of those who take refuge in him! (Psalm 34:8).

Meditation

Think of all the good food you have tasted. God has given us a vast assortment of things to eat, each with a unique taste. I stand in awe of great cooks who can prepare those foods in ways that enhance their tastes.

We are encouraged to taste God, to experience him so deeply that it is like chewing the most delectable dish we've ever had. We taste him now in the wonders of nature, in the closeness of friends and family, and in the fellowship of fellow Christians. We taste Him in the assurance brought by our living Redeemer. And the time is coming when we will taste a new life beyond our imagination, a life with the Source of unutterable bliss.

For Reflection

1. What does it mean to be holy?
2. How can we be more attentive to what Jesus is teaching us in the Bible?
3. What will it be like to be with Jesus in paradise?

Live the Hymn

1. As you read from the Bible today, read slowly, hanging on every word.
2. When you eat, chew slowly, and pay attention to the variety of flavors.. As you eat, think of how good the Lord tastes.

Prayer

Holy Spirit, make us open to the holiness of Jesus today.

Day Thirty-Six:
Love Divine (I)

STANZA ONE

**Love divine, all loves excelling,
Joy of Heav'n to Earth come down,
Fix in us thy humble dwelling,
All thy faithful mercies crown;
Jesus, thou art all compassion,
Pure, unbounded love thou art;
Visit us with thy salvation,
Enter ev'ry trembling heart.**

SCRIPTURE

And may you have the power to understand, as all God's people should, how wide, how long, how high, and how deep his love is (Ephesians 3:18).

MEDITATION

"Love" may be the most debased word in the English language. We use the word to describe our deepest emotions and our most trivial preferences. We say we love our husband, our wife, dogs, movies, dancing, and apple pie. We have lost the depth of the word "love."

But now we come to the deepest and widest love, one that is beyond our greatest fantasy, the divine love that God shows in Jesus who is all compassion. The entire story of the Bible tells of that love. God's people have written countless words reflecting on that love.

How do we react to the Love divine made flesh in Jesus? We pray that God will give us the power to more fully understand that love. And we break out in song to the God who is love.

Stanza Two

Breathe, O breathe thy loving Spirit
Into ev'ry troubled breast;
Let us all in thee inherit,
Let us find thy promised rest;
Take away our love of sinning;
Alpha and Omega be;
End of faith as its beginning,
Set our hearts at liberty.

Scripture

"I am the Alpha and the Omega, the First and the Last, the Beginning and the End" (Revelation 22:13).

Meditation

In almost the last verse of the Bible, Jesus calls Himself by the first and last letters of the Greek alphabet, Alpha and Omega. He is God from "A" to "Z." What does that mean?

Jesus was there at the beginning. He made all things in creation (Colossians 1:16). He is the beginning of God's plan to save humanity. He is the firstborn from the dead, the beginning of a new humanity after his resurrection (Colossians 1:18).

Jesus will be there at the end of the old creation and the beginning of the new heaven and earth (Revelation 21:1).

Jesus is the object of our faith from "A" to "Z." But we look forward to the time when faith becomes sight and we receive our full inheritance as God's children, when Christ is all and in all (Colossians 3:11).

For Reflection

1. Since "love" has lost much of its meaning, what other words can you think of to describe how God has treated us?
2. What are some ways Jesus showed compassion to those around Him?
3. What does it mean that Jesus is the beginning and the end of all things?

Live the Hymn

1. As you pray today, use other words besides "love" to express how God feels about you and you feel about God.
2. Think of Jesus when you first get up and when you go to bed today. Make Him your Alpha and Omega.

Prayer

Love Divine, breathe your Spirit into us today.

Day Thirty-Seven:
Love Divine (II)

STANZA THREE

Come, Almighty to deliver;
Let us all thy grace receive;
Suddenly return, and never,
Never more thy temples leave.
Thee we would be always blessing,
Serve thee as thy host above,
Pray, and praise thee without ceasing,
Glory in thy perfect love.

SCRIPTURE

May your Kingdom come soon. May your will be done on earth, as it is in heaven (Matthew 6:10).

MEDITATION

In the familiar words of the Lord's Prayer, we ask that God's will be done on earth as it is in heaven.

How is God's will done in heaven? The angels do His will completely and immediately. What we pray for is that the same be done on earth. How can that be? We certainly do not see the will of God being done completely and immediately in our day. Instead, it looks as though evil is winning.

This prayer can only be answered by the sudden return of Jesus to earth, bringing the fullness of the kingdom. In the new heaven and earth promised by God, humanity will again commune with Father, Son, and

Spirit in a beautiful garden paradise. God's will for humans, that they will enjoy Him forever, will be completely fulfilled. Then we will praise Him without ceasing, overwhelmed by perfect love.

Stanza Four

Finish, then, thy new creation;
Pure and spotless let us be;
Let us see thy great salvation
Perfectly restored in thee;
Changed from glory into glory
Till in Heav'n we take our place,
Till we cast our crowns before thee,
Lost in wonder, love, and praise!

Scripture

Whenever the living beings give glory and honor and thanks to the one sitting on the throne (the one who lives forever and ever), the twenty-four elders fall down and worship the one sitting on the throne (the one who lives forever and ever). And they lay their crowns before the throne and say,
"You are worthy, O Lord our God,
to receive glory and honor and power.
For you created all things,
and they exist because you created what you pleased" (Revelation 4:9-11).

Meditation

The book of Revelation mentions the twenty-four elders several times (Revelation (4:4, 10; 5:5, 6, 8, 11, 14; 7:11, 13; 11:16; 14:3; and 19:4). Who are these elders? The interpretation that makes the most sense to me is that they represent the twelve tribes of Israel and the twelve apostles. If so, the elders stand for all the people of God throughout the ages. The crowns they wear show they are leaders in God's kingdom. Yet they throw down their crowns before the throne of the eternal God to show that He alone is the true King.

The hymn pictures all who trust in Jesus as kings under Him. We proclaim Him Lord by casting our crowns at the foot of the throne of the One who lives forever. We do that daily now, but the day will come when we do it ultimately in the finished new creation.

For Reflection

1. What will it be like when Jesus returns?
2. What will it be like to praise Jesus forever? How do you think we will praise Him?
3. What does it mean to cast our crowns before Jesus?

Live the Hymn

1. In silence, meditate on the love of God.
2. Today imagine yourself wearing a crown showing that Jesus has made you a king over his people. Then imagine taking off the crown and placing it at the feet of Jesus.

Prayer

Love Divine, fill us today as your temples.

Day Thirty-Eight:
O For a Thousand Tongues to Sing (I)

STANZA ONE

O for a thousand tongues to sing,
My dear Redeemer's praise!
The glories of my God and King,
The triumphs of his grace!

SCRIPTURE

Then I looked again, and I heard the voices of thousands and millions of angels around the throne and of the living beings and the elders. And they sang in a mighty chorus:
"Worthy is the Lamb who was slaughtered—
to receive power and riches
and wisdom and strength
and honor and glory and blessing" (Revelation 5:11-13).

MEDITATION

Here Wesley's hymn reflects another vision from Revelation where more than a thousand tongues of angels, humans, and other creatures praise Jesus as the Lamb of God.

The New Testament, especially the Book of Revelation, pictures Jesus as the one who triumphs over evil. Unlike the old westerns or war movies that win the battle with a faster gun or larger army, Jesus defeats evil as a slain Lamb. He wins the war through self-sacrificial love.

In the end, it's not the most violent warrior who wins but it is grace that triumphs.

Stanza Two

My gracious Master, and my God,
Assist me to proclaim,
To spread through all the earth abroad,
The honors of thy name.

Scripture

I am in chains now, still preaching this message as God's ambassador. So pray that I will keep on speaking boldly for him, as I should (Ephesians 6:20).

Meditation

We usually think of Paul as the courageous apostle who preaches with conviction, even when it means he will suffer for his proclamation. But Paul was under great pressure to keep quiet about the good news of Jesus. Prison has a way of making one cautious about what you say and do.

If Paul needed prayers so he could boldly speak for God, so do we. Even though we are not in chains, the looks we get from those around us when we talk about Jesus might move us to silence. Yes, we want a thousand tongues to sing the praise of our Redeemer, but sometimes we need God's assistance so we can proclaim the name of Jesus with the one tongue we have.

Stanza Three

Jesus, the name that charms our fears,
That bids our sorrows cease;

'Tis music in the sinner's ears,
'Tis life, and health, and peace.

Scripture

"I am leaving you with a gift—peace of mind and heart. And the peace I give is a gift the world cannot give. So don't be troubled or afraid" (John 14:27).

Meditation

"Don't be afraid."

When I hear those words, I get nervous. To hear them means that something is wrong, something I might be afraid of.

If the one who says those words has already taken care of the problem, then all is well. "An unauthorized charge has been made to your account, but you are not responsible for the payment." "Your blood test at first came back positive, but we re-tested and all is well." "We checked the warning light on your car, but nothing was wrong, so we reset it."

Jesus charms our more serious fears—fears of meaninglessness, rejection, shame, and even death. Those fears are fleeting in light of His gifts of life, health, and peace.

For Reflection

1. How does grace triumph over evil?
2. What makes you reluctant to tell others about Jesus?
3. What are you most afraid of?

Live the Hymn

1. Show the grace of Jesus today in an act of service to someone.
2. When you are afraid today, say the name of Jesus and know He removes fear.

Prayer

Jesus, we praise your Name as the one who removes all our fears.

Day Thirty-Nine:
O For a Thousand Tongues to Sing (II)

STANZA FOUR

He breaks the Power of cancell'd sin,
He sets the pris'ner free;
His blood can make the foulest clean;
His blood availed me.

SCRIPTURE

He canceled the record of the charges against us and took it away by nailing it to the cross (Colossians 2:14).

MEDITATION

"That charge has been cancelled." That's good news when you've been charged for something you did not purchase.

It's even better news when you are not charged for something you did buy but shouldn't have.

We use the word "charge" for financial transactions, but it is much more serious if we are charged with a crime. Then we want the charge to be cancelled and the record expunged as though it never happened.

That's exactly what Jesus did for us on the cross. And He cancelled the charges against us, not because we were innocent, but because we were guilty. Cancelling them cost Him His life.

Yet even after the record of our sins has been cancelled, we still sometimes feel the power of guilt and shame. Jesus breaks the power of the sin He cancelled, completely setting us free.

Stanza Five

He speaks, and, list'ning to his Voice,
New Life the Dead receive;
The mournful broken Hearts rejoice,
The humble Poor believe.

Scripture

Jesus told them, "Go back to John and tell him what you have heard and seen— the blind see, the lame walk, those with leprosy are cured, the deaf hear, the dead are raised to life, and the Good News is being preached to the poor" (Matthew 11:4-5).

Meditation

John the Baptist points to Jesus and says, "Look! The Lamb of God who takes away the sin of the world!" (John 1:29). John had absolute conviction.

Then he loses it. He finds himself in prison, awaiting death, and he wonders why Jesus has not yet revealed Himself as Messiah. He wonders, "Did I get it all wrong?" So he sends a message to Jesus, "Are you the Messiah we've been expecting, or should we keep looking for someone else?" (Matthew 11:3). Jesus replies by listing all the things that God is doing through Jesus as the Messiah.

Are we like John? We started with full conviction in Jesus, wanting to praise Him with a thousand tongues, but now life seems to go on the way it always has. Everything remains the same. Nothing gets better. We question our faith.

Jesus says, "Open your eyes and look." See what Jesus has done and is still doing.

It is not wrong to doubt, but we must doubt our doubts. Jesus says, "God blesses those who do not fall away because of me" (Matthew 11:6).

Stanza Six

**Look unto him, ye nations, own
Your God, ye fallen race;
Look, and be sav'd through faith alone,
Be justify'd by grace!**

Scripture

For you were slaughtered, and your blood has ransomed people for God from every tribe and language and people and nation (Revelation 5:9).

Meditation

All patriots love their country and think it is the best. There's nothing wrong with that. But some think their country is morally superior to others or even closer to God than others.

God chose Israel to be His people. He did that out of grace. He never intended for the Israelites to think that they alone were God's nation. He called them to be a light to other nations.

So today we must not think of our country as a new Israel, somehow closer to God than all others. Instead, we remember that we have a new citizenship that includes those from every nation. Jesus calls those in every country to look to Him, to acknowledge Him as their only Lord, and to be justified by grace through faith.

For Reflection

1. How does it feel to have charges cancelled?
2. What is the answer to doubt?
3. Which country is God's country?

Live the Hymn

1. As you pray today, open your hands to let go of all the cancelled sin and shame.
2. Look for the work of Jesus around you today.

Prayer

Healing and life-giving Jesus, open our eyes to your work in every nation.

Day Forty:
A Charge to Keep

STANZA ONE

A charge to keep I have;
A God to glorify;
A never-dying soul to save,
And fit it for the sky:

SCRIPTURE

I charge you in the presence of God and of Christ Jesus, who is to judge the living and the dead, and by his appearing and his kingdom: preach the word; be ready in season and out of season; reprove, rebuke, and exhort, with complete patience and teaching (2 Timothy 4:1-2, ESV).

MEDITATION

In *O For a Thousand Tongues*, we saw how Jesus has cancelled the charges against us, freeing us from sin.

This hymn uses the word "charge" in a different way, not as accusation of sin but as a solemn obligation. All of Charles Wesley's hymns emphasize salvation by grace through faith. Nothing we do can earn our salvation. But God created us in His image so we can respond to His grace and love. This hymn calls for that wholehearted response.

Thus, while it is God alone who in Christ saves our "never-dying soul," we also have a call to let Jesus do His saving work through us.

Stanza Two

**To serve the present age,
My calling to fulfill;
O may it all my pow'rs engage,
To do my Master's will!**

Scripture

Therefore I, a prisoner for serving the Lord, beg you to lead a life worthy of your calling, for you have been called by God (Ephesians 4:1).

Meditation

What is your calling?

I'm known Christians who obsessed over their calling, wondering if God was calling them to another place and a greater ministry.

Your calling is what you are doing right now. You might have a calling as a husband or wife or child or parent or boss or employee. God has placed us where He wants us. What He asks us to do is to serve those around us.

And we are to serve with all our powers, giving honest effort while relying on the power of God.

Stanza Three

**Arm me with jealous care
As in thy sight to live;
And oh! thy servant, Lord, prepare,
A strict account to give.**

SCRIPTURE

"Then the servant with the one bag of silver came and said, 'Master, I knew you were a harsh man, harvesting crops you didn't plant and gathering crops you didn't cultivate. I was afraid I would lose your money, so I hid it in the earth. Look, here is your money back.'" (Matthew 25:24-25).

MEDITATION

In what is usually called "the parable of the talents" (Matthew 25:14-30), God is pictured as a wealthy man who entrusts his money to servants while he is off on a trip. God condemns the servant who only returns what he was given, calling him wicked and lazy.

Is God harsh and strict, hoping to catch us in a fault? No! God is love. But because He loves us, He wants us to be good and faithful servants.

It's a bad parent who withholds love from their child until the child meets a certain standard. On the other hand, parents who love their children unconditionally still want those children to be the best version of themselves that they can possibly be.

So also with God. Our Father loves us with a fierce and strict love.

STANZA FOUR

Help me to watch and pray,
And, on thyself rely;
Assur'd, if I my trust betray,
I shall forever die.

SCRIPTURE

Work hard to show the results of your salvation, obeying God with deep reverence and fear. For God is working in you, giving you the desire and the power to do what pleases him (Philippians 2:12-13).

Meditation

Are we working hard for God or is He doing His work in us?

The clear answer of the Bible is, "Yes!"

God calls us to be His co-workers. So much so, that it is impossible to say when we are doing the work or God is doing the work. That's why, when we are working hard for Jesus, we are relying on Him to do the work. As we serve, we always watch and pray.

And what if we don't? "I shall forever die."

It seems a terrible way to end a hymn (or a book). It was so offensive to some that later hymnbooks changed the words to:

O let me not my trust betray,

But press to realms on high.

These words are an appropriate ending to reflections on the hymns of Charles Wesley, because they show the seriousness of God's love for us. The grace that Wesley celebrates in his hymns is not a cheap grace that calls for a weak response from us. No, the full-bodied grace of God, shown in Jesus and placed in us by the Spirit, calls us to complete trust. A trust we dare not betray. A trust in the Source of Life. A trust that has eternal consequences.

For Reflection

1. Do we save our souls or does Jesus?
2. Does grace make us less likely to keep the charge we have or more likely to keep it?
3. How do we know that the calling we have from God is a serious charge?

Live the Hymn

1. Reflect on the Wesley hymn you like the most.
2. As you work today, think of God working in you.

PRAYER

God of love, give us the strength to keep the charge you have given us for this day.

About

Kharis Publishing:

Kharis Publishing, an imprint of Kharis Media LLC, is a leading Christian and inspirational book publisher based in Aurora, Chicago metropolitan area, Illinois. Kharis' dual mission is to give voice to under-represented writers (including women and first-time authors) and equip orphans in developing countries with literacy tools. That is why, for each book sold, the publisher channels some of the proceeds into providing books and computers for orphanages in developing countries so that these kids may learn to read, dream, and grow. For a limited time, Kharis Publishing is accepting unsolicited queries for nonfiction (Christian, self-help, memoirs, business, health and wellness) from qualified leaders, professionals, pastors, and ministers. Learn more at: https://kharispublishing.com/

www.ingramcontent.com/pod-product-compliance
Lightning Source LLC
Chambersburg PA
CBHW070156100426
42743CB00013B/2932